The Complete Guide to Investing in

Duplexes, Triplexes, Fourplexes, and Mobile Homes:

What Smart Investors Need to Know Explained Simply

By E.E. Mazier

THE COMPLETE GUIDE TO INVESTING IN DUPLEXES, TRIPLEXES, FOURPLEXES, AND MOBILE HOMES: WHAT SMART INVESTORS NEED TO KNOW EXPLAINED SIMPLY

Copyright © 2009 by Atlantic Publishing Group, Inc.
1405 SW 6th Ave. • Ocala, Florida 34471 • 800-814-1132 • 352-622-1875—Fax
Web site: www.atlantic-pub.com • E-mail: sales@atlantic-pub.com
SAN Number: 268-1250

ISBN-13: 978-1-60138-206-1   ISBN-10: 1-60138-206-5

Library of Congress Cataloging-in-Publication Data

Mazier, E. E., 1953-
  The complete guide to investing in duplexes, triplexes, fourplexes,
and mobile homes : what smart investors need to know explained simply /
by E.E. Mazier.
      p. cm.
  Includes bibliographical references and index.
  ISBN-13: 978-1-60138-206-1 (alk. paper)
  ISBN-10: 1-60138-206-5 (alk. paper)
  1. Real estate investment--United States. 2. Apartment
houses--Purchasing--United States. 3. Residential real estate--United
States. 4. Mobile homes--United States--Purchasing. I. Title.

  HD259.M38 2008
  332.63'243--dc22
                        2008032618

INTERIOR LAYOUT DESIGN: Nicole Deck ndeck@atlantic-pub.com

Printed in the United States

We recently lost our beloved pet "Bear," who was not only our best and dearest friend but also the "Vice President of Sunshine" here at Atlantic Publishing. He did not receive a salary but worked tirelessly 24 hours a day to please his parents. Bear was a rescue dog that turned around and showered myself, my wife Sherri, his grandparents

Jean, Bob and Nancy and every person and animal he met (maybe not rabbits) with friendship and love. He made a lot of people smile every day.

We wanted you to know that a portion of the profits of this book will be donated to The Humane Society of the United States. *–Douglas & Sherri Brown*

The human-animal bond is as old as human history. We cherish our animal companions for their unconditional affection and acceptance. We feel a thrill when we glimpse wild creatures in their natural habitat or in our own backyard.

Unfortunately, the human-animal bond has at times been weakened. Humans have exploited some animal species to the point of extinction.

The Humane Society of the United States makes a difference in the lives of animals here at home and worldwide. The HSUS is dedicated to creating a world where our relationship with animals is guided by compassion. We seek a truly humane society in which animals are respected for their intrinsic value, and where the human-animal bond is strong.

Want to help animals? We have plenty of suggestions. Adopt a pet from a local shelter, join The Humane Society and be a part of our work to help companion animals and wildlife. You will be funding our educational, legislative, investigative and outreach projects in the U.S. and across the globe.

Or perhaps you'd like to make a memorial donation in honor of a pet, friend or relative? You can through our Kindred Spirits program. And if you'd like to contribute in a more structured way, our Planned Giving Office has suggestions about estate planning, annuities, and even gifts of stock that avoid capital gains taxes.

Maybe you have land that you would like to preserve as a lasting habitat for wildlife. Our Wildlife Land Trust can help you. Perhaps the land you want to share is a backyard— that's enough. Our Urban Wildlife Sanctuary Program will show you how to create a habitat for your wild neighbors.

So you see, it's easy to help animals. And The HSUS is here to help.

2100 L Street NW • Washington, DC 20037 • 202-452-1100 www.hsus.org

DEDICATION

To Carmine: You are the best partner I could have hoped for in life.
Thank you for all that you give me every day.

To Aura: Thank you for insisting that I stand
on my own two feet and watch out for myself.

TABLE OF CONTENTS

INTRODUCTION

You may have said to yourself, "If I had only invested in real estate when prices were low, I would be sitting pretty right now." You may accept your mediocre economic lot in life because you think it is too late to learn how to find and invest in good properties.

It is not. If you are armed with the right information, it is never too late for you to start building wealth and financial security by investing in residential properties, such as duplexes, triplexes, fourplexes, and mobile homes (now known as "manufactured homes" — see Chapter 11 for more detail on different types of these homes).

The economy of a nation is cyclical, with booms followed by busts. Periods of tremendous opportunities to build wealth by investing in rising stocks and launching new businesses inevitably are followed by periods when stock prices drop hard and businesses lay off employees by the thousands and even shut down. If those opportunities were so wonderful in the first place, it is hard to fathom why so many people lose money when the economy goes bust.

One reason is that even in good times, it is not easy to pick a stock. To reduce your risk, you need to know how to read a company's financial statements, how that company compares with others in the same industry, how the background and experience of those running the company measure up, and whether the company is facing the possibility of investigation by a government agency or a state attorney general or litigation by consumers injured by its products. Most of this information is not easy to dig up or to dig through, yet you need to know it before plunking down your hard-earned cash to buy stock in any company, even if it is a Fortune 500 company. Also, you have to keep monitoring the company so that you can judge whether the time is right to sell your stock or buy more.

Operating your own business is another difficult venture. In this age of big-box, one-stop-shopping behemoths, small retailers are being squeezed out of existence. In addition, many businesses fail within the first few years. The problem is that many people who start their own small businesses do so without understanding the market they are entering, developing a solid business plan, establishing a network of business relationships, or investing enough in appropriate advertising vehicles. Add to this the numerous challenges involved in finding, keeping, and managing trustworthy employees; dealing with taxes, government licensing, and inspection requirements; and putting in the necessary long hours, and it quickly becomes evident that owning your own business is not the easy or surefire way to build wealth. It may even leave you poorer.

Although many outside factors also come into play, it is the lack of proper preparation that causes many investors to lose money when the stock market dives and businesses go belly up. The steep ascents and descents of the national economy can feel like a nightmarish roller coaster ride that never ends, but your personal finances do not have to be on a circular track of lifts and dips. You can take steps to protect yourself, to smooth out the ride, and to arrive at a point well beyond where you started.

One of the most reliable, enduring ways to do this is by investing in real estate. There are several reasons for this. One reason is that land normally holds its value over a long period of time. Another reason is that you do not need an advanced education to learn how to find a decent property, finance it, and manage it with the end goal of putting money in your pocket. It is also true that no matter what shape the national economy happens to be in, people always need a place to live, and not everyone can or wants to buy a home.

Buying one or more properties may seem as intimidating as buying stock in a company or opening a store. The truth is that if you are prepared and have done your homework, there is no reason why you cannot make a smart purchase of land with a residential structure on it or of a nice mobile home. Moreover, with a good understanding and a decent plan, you do not have to work 24/7 to reach your financial goals, because what you purchase will work for you every day.

This book will show you that much of what is involved in investing in duplexes, triplexes, fourplexes, and mobile homes is based on logic and common sense. Like anything else worthwhile, investing in these types of properties requires time and patience to learn the fundamentals. You can do this by reading and studying the information in this book and, more important, by using that information as a springboard to buying your first duplex, triplex, fourplex, or mobile home.

How to Use This Book

The goals of this book are twofold. The first is to give you the information you need to make sensible investments in residential properties that are appropriate for your particular situation and the dreams that you have in mind. The second goal is to encourage you to apply your newly acquired knowledge and move from dreaming to going out to find and buy properties.

This book is aimed at the first-time investor as well as the investor who already owns a one-family rental property. A person who already owns a one-family investment property has taken an important first step in securing his or her financial freedom. These people may as well kick it up a notch and start building wealth faster by investing in properties with two to four units or even in mobile homes.

The chapters that follow cover the benefits of owning multifamily housing units and mobile homes; creating wealth through real estate and mobile homes; finding, financing, and selling good properties; maintaining properties; dealing with tenants and vacancies; and navigating taxation, zoning, and regulatory challenges.

A good strategy is to initially read this book the whole way through. This will give you an overview of the realities, challenges, and opportunities involved in investing in residential properties. Then, as you go through the process of finding, evaluating, purchasing, and managing properties, you can refer back to the detailed pointers in the chapters that correspond to the steps that you are taking.

This book also includes Case Studies that contain real-life tips to remember and pitfalls to avoid from investors, attorneys, and other experts. This feature is presented to help guide you on your path to becoming the savvy and successful real estate investor that you want to be.

Study, Reflect, and Act

The Small Business Administration (SBA) has reported that many people spend years in the process of starting up a business but never launch it.

Additionally, many have heard that the key to financial success is to "make money work for you." Yet, most people continue to work for money.

There are a few reasons that so many capable individuals who have dreams of success on their terms, and who should be well on the road to financial security, continue to struggle to make ends meet and are living paycheck to paycheck.

The answer can lie in fear, procrastination, indecision, and listening to naysayers, which can all stem from self-doubt.

Successful people have learned to quiet those doubts. They know they no longer have time to be sidetracked by negative thoughts. They are too busy making their plans and, more important, implementing those plans. In other words, they have learned how to get out of their own way and put themselves on a track to success.

You can read this book and other books on real estate investment, and you can spend good money attending seminars or buying DVDs and audio CDs on this subject. Yet, you will not buy that first multiunit residential property or mobile home if you insist on not taking any risks. The result will be no progress in achieving your financial goals.

Alternatively, you can study the information in this book, develop an understanding of the principles explained, and then hunt down that first duplex or mobile home. When the title papers are in your hand and the checks start rolling in, you can look at yourself in the mirror and say, "I am on my way. Hurray for me."

Part I

REAL ESTATE AS AN INVESTMENT

1

WHY REAL ESTATE
BEATS OTHER INVESTMENTS

There are many ways to invest money. These include stocks, corporate and municipal bonds, government securities, collateralized debt obligations, mortgage-backed securities, mutual funds, and exchange traded funds, to name just a few. It is easy to buy into most, if not all, of these investment products. But without sufficient understanding of how the products operate and of the particular industries and companies that they each encompass, an investor cannot select wisely among the dizzying array of products while determining how best to reduce risk. Even if an investment is chosen carefully and with knowledge of the fundamentals involved, a return on investment is not guaranteed, and the money invested may be lost on many of the riskier products.

There are more conservative investment vehicles, such as money markets, certificates of deposit, and that reliable bank savings account. Although the principal invested in these vehicles is never lost, the interest rates are sluggish and frequently much lower than the rates of return from other types of investments. It is hard to get rich with money market funds, certificates of deposit, savings accounts, and other risk-free investments.

A survey commissioned by the Consumer Federation of America and Wachovia Corporation in late 2007 revealed that 52 percent of Americans believe that they are not saving enough for retirement, 35 percent believe that what they are saving is inadequate to cover their short- and long-term financial needs, and 17 percent cannot afford to put anything away in savings.

Many of those who are trying to build a nest egg for their retirement are pinning their futures on the performance of the investment products previously mentioned. Pensions, 401(k)s, and individual retirement accounts commonly are invested in one or more of those products. With market fluctuations, falling stock prices, company bankruptcies, and employers reneging on their promises to provide their workers with fully funded pension plans, many hardworking people are anxious. They are starting to realize that their future security, which is in the hands of others, is either in jeopardy or nonexistent.

An investment that does not allow you to enjoy the fruits of your labor, keeps you in a state of anxiety because of factors beyond your control, and is controlled by others who do not know you and do not care about your financial needs and goals is of little value.

Investing in residential properties is an excellent alternative to high-risk or sluggish investment vehicles. As will be seen in the chapters to come, an investor in residential properties is able to select his or her own comfort level of risk.

Kim McGregor invests in duplexes in Texas. He admitted that he is not a gambler, which is why real estate is the investment vehicle that has sparked his interest for more than 30 years. He said he enjoys the degree of control that investing in residential properties allows him, and he has first-hand knowledge of what happens when retirement money is placed in the hands of others.

"I had a little bit of money in WorldComm when it went out of business. I received one of those infamous letters from a stockbroker saying, 'In respect to the IRS, this stock is now deemed worthless.' So that is what I got for my $2,000 IRA investment. It is hard for that to happen in real estate."

Investing in residential properties is a proven, reliable way to achieve financial security because its basics are easy to master, because people always need a place to live, and — in terms of investing in real estate — because land is a finite commodity. More specifically, because the United States, even with its wide open spaces, has a limited amount of land available for housing.

It is true that real estate is a cyclical business. Although prices can rise continuously over several years, they also can get caught in a downward trend, as is occurring in many parts of the country now, in 2008. Nevertheless, the savvy real estate investor is not frightened by price drops. He or she (or it, if a partnership or corporation) has paid as little as possible for a property and therefore knows that he or she is in a good position when prices start to climb again. The investor has listened to the old adage of "buy low, sell high," which also applies to many other types of investments. The savvy real estate investor also knows that a period of price reductions may be the perfect time to pick up desirable properties that were out of reach when prices were high.

The focus of this book is duplexes, triplexes, fourplexes (also known as "quadraplexes" or "quads"), and mobile homes. For purposes of financing, houses that consist of two to four units are considered residential multifamily properties, while houses that have five or more units are classified as commercial. Mobile homes are now referred to in the industry as manufactured homes, and they are not the run-down, cramped trailers of days gone by. Nor are they in the same category as real estate. Instead, as will be further examined in Chapter 11, buying and selling a mobile home is more akin to buying and selling a personal item, such as an automobile. On the other hand, a mobile-home park is land that is bought and sold like real estate, at times together with mobile homes that are in the park.

By investing in residential real estate, particularly in duplexes, triplexes, and fourplexes and also mobile homes and mobile-home parks, you take direct control of your investment dollars. Investing in these types of properties allows you to build up your monthly income, reduce the amount of income taxes you pay, and accumulate real wealth — which is having enough money after the bills are paid to do what you want to do. It could be to move to a warmer climate after the children have grown, travel to the land of your ancestors, do volunteer work, run for public office, or even start a new business.

Investing in Real Estate Means Owning Your Own Business

Investing in real estate (and mobile homes) is itself a business and must be treated as such by those who are serious about succeeding at it. This means having a grasp of the principles and dynamics involved, keeping adequate records, reviewing the state of your assets, and revising your investment goals periodically. It also means, as in any business, being on the lookout for new opportunities to make money. The beauty of investing in real estate is that an ordinary person can learn the ins and outs of the business without a degree or special schooling.

The spirit of entrepreneurship, the urge to have one's own business, is strong in the United States. Some people dream of opening a business where they can provide the same type of product or service that they do as when they are someone else's employee. Others see owning their own business as the best way to a life they could not otherwise attain because of language, educational, or other barriers. Yet, others endure their working years with pleasant thoughts of owning a small shop when they retire.

The SBA reports that, every year, about 7 percent of the people of working age actively engage in efforts to start a business. Within two years, about a third of those efforts results in the launch of a business. About six million new businesses are started each year.

It is well known that many businesses that are launched will fail. Experts cite failure rates as high as 40 percent within the first year and between 33 percent and 50 percent within the initial five years that a business is started.

The most recent available figures from the SBA indicate that fewer businesses were launched (called "firm births" by the SBA) in 2006 than in 2005 and that more businesses were terminated in 2006 than in the previous year. The SBA reports that terminations are due not only to closings, but also to mergers and buyouts. (**Note:** The sharp drop in bankruptcies for 2006 may be due to statutory changes enacted by Congress to set higher standards for qualifying for a bankruptcy.)

FIRM BIRTHS		FIRM TERMINATIONS		BUSINESS BANKRUPTCIES	
2005	2006	2005	2006	2005	2006
U.S. total					
653,100e.*	649,700e.	543,700e.	564,900e.	39,201	19,695
*e= estimate (From the SBA, Office of Advocacy, "The Small Business Economy for Data Year 2006: A Report to the President.")					

There are many reasons why small businesses fail. The SBA has suggested that entrepreneurs may not understand the business model of their particular enterprise; in other words, they may be unaware of the necessary prescription for making money. Therefore, while many entrepreneurs may succeed in starting new businesses, they may lack the crucial understanding of how to grow and develop their businesses into enduring, profitable ventures with positive cash flows.

A lack of adequate cash flow means that not enough money enters a business to allow it to pay all the bills, let alone to return a profit to the owner. It is hard for many small business owners to project how much money will come in every month. Without a proper cash flow projection, it is virtually impossible to figure out how much can be spent every month or to know how and when the business can be expanded.

Another reason small businesses fail is that they often start with or hit on a good idea that works for them, such as a particular product or service, and they keep going with that idea. The owners fail to diversify and to come up with new products or services. After a while, business stagnates. Similarly, stagnation, and even contraction, will occur if a business fails to expand its customer base.

The problems of inadequate cash flow, failure to diversify, and failure to expand the customer base can be avoided when investing in real estate.

Cash flow: An investor who has done his or her due diligence knows how much the monthly expenses of a duplex, triplex, fourplex, or mobile home will be; how much the rent is; and how much will be left over after the expenses are paid from the monthly rents. The investor also has included in his or her calculations a cushion for the unforeseen broken water heater, collapsed chimney, or other unexpected expenses.

Diversification: After an investor has found a formula that works for his or her particular circumstances — such as owning three or four duplexes that are fully rented and buying and selling one or two properties a year for a quick turnover — the investor does not need to tinker with his or her winning formula. Another way of diversifying is by owning some large, more expensive properties and some smaller, less expensive ones. Lower-priced properties do not drop much in price during a price bust, while more expensive properties rise higher in price during a boom. Thus, lower-priced properties offer the investor safety, while more expensive properties offer vast profit potential.

Customer base: If the properties are in areas of high demand, there will always be a steady availability of renters from which to choose. Plus, if the investor is careful to select responsible, financially stable tenants, he or she may not need to look for new ones for a long time.

Benefits of Multiunit Residences and Mobile Homes

The coming chapters of this book will examine the intricacies of successfully investing in duplexes, triplexes, fourplexes, and mobile homes. For the purposes of this section, it is enough to understand that owning such properties and having them rented is a sound way of receiving income every month and seeing their value rise over time. Moreover, the investor who leverages — meaning that he or she puts little money down and finances most of the purchase price of a property — will learn enough from this book to know how to do the calculations to have a positive cash flow. At the same time, the equity will grow as the mortgage loan is paid down and the value of the property appreciates.

Lisa Moren-Bromma has been a real estate investor for 30 years. She has owned one- and two-family houses, a mobile-home park, and commercial properties. Even in the current difficult market, she remains enthusiastic about the prospects for investors.

"Being creative makes a real estate investor money, and with the market conditions as they are, I believe that if you know what you are doing and you can figure out how to get the right quality of tenants, you will be just fine. I am talking about properties for the long term. In this market, I would not even consider buying properties for the short term."

In real estate and mobile-home ownership, the investor is the one who controls how expensive the investment property should be. If an investor is starting out with extremely little money and requires cash flow, he or she can buy a less expensive property that will generate most of the profit in the form of cash flow. Conversely, if the investor has income from another, primary source, such as from a profession, and he or she chooses to buy higher-priced, better properties, more of the profits will come in the form of long-term capital gain, which will be taxed at a lower rate. In addition, the tax benefits of buying a property with little money down and most of the price financed can offset the tax on income received from other sources.

At first glance, it might seem more profitable and more manageable to own one building with five or more apartments in it. It is true that the price of an apartment unit in a building can diminish as the size of the building increases. Nonetheless, there are several important considerations. First, by investing in several properties with fewer units, the investor can buy some for cash flow and others for the tax benefits that they offer today. An investor who buys less expensive properties can sell them and then reinvest the profits in the higher-priced properties while deferring the payment of the capital gains tax.

Second, you can lose an element of control over a building if you have several tenants living in it. One reason is that certain tenant protection statutes kick in as soon as you have more than three or four apartments in a building. In such a case, you have to follow strict statutory requirements about the type and timing of notices that you must give tenants whom you want to evict for not paying the rent or for creating a hazard or a nuisance. A building with multiple apartments may also be subject to local rent-control or rent-stabilization ordinances that limit how much the rent can be raised each year, even if the owner has made substantial repairs in the building, such as putting in a new furnace or a new roof.

Another way that an owner loses complete control over a larger residential property is that tenants who live in multiunit apartment buildings are more likely to run into each other daily and to complain to each other about the rent or about perceived faults in their apartments or in other parts of the building. If those tenants get angry enough, they could band together and organize rent strikes or take you, the landlord, to court to demand improvements in their building. Investors who find themselves in court repeatedly, for protracted periods of time, or who must pay lawyers to represent them in litigation will soon see their profits evaporate.

In contrast, renters who live apart from each other in separate, discrete duplexes, in mobile homes, or even in triplexes and fourplexes most likely would not know the tenants in other properties and would not be involved with each others' daily affairs. This makes it much less likely that they would organize against the owner.

A third advantage of buying duplexes, triplexes, and fourplexes is that properties of one to four units fit in the residential-loan category of most lenders. This can be a terrific deal for the beginning investor, because he or she may be able to finance a property with a conventional loan that requires a down payment as low as 5 to 10 percent. There are also loan-guarantee programs for the first-time home buyer through mortgage lenders and the Federal Housing Authority (FHA) that allow as little as a 3 percent down payment, as long as the owner lives in one of the units.

Regarding mobile homes, the industry has worked hard to improve the image of mobile-home parks from that of haphazard collections of run-down, unsafe trailers. Today, the better-run parks sport attractive landscaping and amenities, such as volleyball courts and barbecue grills. The homes themselves have improved through better manufacturing techniques. New mobile homes cost much less than new houses, and they require little maintenance. The homes can be set on private property or on leased property. If placed on leased property, there is no land-purchase expense. Moreover, property taxes are lower than for a house or an apartment building, as are the utility costs.

Finally, from a tenant's point of view, the most desirable aspect of living in duplexes, triplexes, fourplexes, and mobile homes is the increased sense of privacy. Living in units that are stacked upon each other, apartment dwellers may view and treat their places as temporary way stations. In contrast, tenants in duplexes, triplexes, fourplexes, and mobile homes can enjoy a greater sense of living in a single-family home, and they often take better care of their units. The rent for a duplex, triplex, fourplex, or mobile home is on average higher than for an apartment (but lower than for single-family houses), and yet, tenants are willing to pay more for that sense of privacy and for a homey touch, such as a porch, a back yard, or a deck. Plus, if the units on a lot can be fenced off and each tenant made responsible for his own yard, the owner will have the added bonus of being alleviated of lawn-maintenance and gardening expenses.

This Is Not a Get-Rich-Quick Scheme

As you read through the chapters ahead and acquire an understanding of how investing in residential real estate and mobile homes works, take note that this is not an investment vehicle for those looking to make a fast buck, contrary to the impression given by late-night infomercials.

It may be possible to occasionally flip a property (sell quickly for a profit). Though, broadly speaking, you must take your time and exercise patience when building wealth through investing in real estate and mobile homes. Treat it as a business and be guided by sound principles and judgment based on your growing knowledge of the business, and you can minimize the risk of failure while increasing your personal fortune.

CASE STUDY: ANNA MILLS

President,
Toledo Real Estate Investors Association
(419) 283-8427
www.ToledoREIA.com

I was a secretary in a real estate agency before I became a licensed real estate agent more than 30 years ago. About a year later, I began investing in single-family homes. I now manage my houses and fourplexes for my business partner.

My three great fears when I started investing were vacancies, repairs, and liquidity. Over the years I began doing my own repairs. To learn how, I would get videos from the library or sub out to a contractor and learn from him. Eventually I became a licensed electrical, plumbing, and heating contractor in Ohio and a general contractor in Michigan. So the repairs never became a problem, and problems with liquidity and vacancies never materialized. What you fear is what you don't know, and the things that worry you the most are what you go educate yourself on.

If I had been less fearful, I would have invested in multifamily properties. If you have a vacancy in them, the rents from the other units can cover the operating expenses. I would not have wasted those years when I was young just trying to cope with a couple of single-family properties.

The real value plays in multiunits are the fixer-uppers, where you can go in and fix small problems of deferred maintenance. The second type of value play is where you buy low but have high expenses, such as for insulation or storm windows. The third value play is low occupancy, where the numbers indicate that you could bring in renters and make a difference in the return.

My advice to those starting out as investors in rental properties is: (1) confirm what the actual numbers are for properties you consider, (2) look at the neighborhood comparables to get an idea of how the neighborhood is doing, (3) build a good team of professionals, (4) network with others who invest in rentals, and (5) don't be so fearful.

2

THE COMPONENTS OF RETURN ON INVESTMENT

The fundamental reason that a person puts money into an investment is to obtain a return on investment (ROI). This is true for investments in stocks and bonds, mutual funds, certificates of deposit, and, of course, real estate.

These are the components of ROI in real estate investments:

1) Cash flow

2) Appreciation

3) Equity growth through loan reduction

4) Tax benefits

It is crucial to understand each of these components to be able to calculate each and to understand how they all relate to each other. It is this knowledge that will allow you to run the numbers and decide whether a particular property is worth your time, money, and effort. This, in turn, will allow you to reduce your exposure to risky ventures and increase your chances of success.

The calculation of ROI is part of a real estate investor's due diligence, which is the thorough research, verification, and analysis of the relevant data, projections, and representations about a property. Much of this is conducted before offering to buy a property, but there are important steps that also must be taken between the signing of a contract and the closing of title. Due diligence includes running the numbers as well as appraising and inspecting the property. Due diligence is so vital that an entire chapter, Chapter 8, is devoted to it in this book.

As you continue reading, bear in mind that each component of ROI can vary significantly from state to state and even from neighborhood to neighborhood. One area may offer a high cash flow but a lower return from appreciation in value. Another area may offer good value appreciation but few tax benefits.

Cash Flow

Cash flow is the money that remains after the bills have been paid. It may be:

- Allowed to accumulate in an account

- Reinvested in the property that produced it in the form of upkeep or upgrade

- Used in a leveraged purchase of another investment property

- Put into the pocket of the investor as profit

The calculation of cash flow from a residential property is fairly uncomplicated, as long as all relevant information is available. An investor who is considering the purchase of a rental property should insist on having all the relevant data and should be prepared to walk away from a deal if data are withheld.

The most important figures that an investor must have to calculate cash flow are the annual gross income of the property, annual expenses of operating the property, and total debt load on the investor's loan(s) to finance the property.

Gross Annual Income

Gross annual income is the total amount of rents collected at the target property in a year. This figure will change if the rents are increased each year. An investor who is considering a property must insist on seeing the rent roll, which is the schedule of rent paid over time for the units on the property.

Annual Operating Expenses

Annual operating expenses are what some sellers try to obscure or distort to make their property seem more profitable than it is. These are the expenses for real property taxes, nonresident owner's insurance on the property, maintenance, and repair charges. There are also a variety of other expenses that may apply, depending on local governmental requirements and the terms of the landlord/tenant lease, such as heating charges, water charges, sewer charges, miscellaneous government fees (such as landlord's registration fee), utilities in common areas, garbage removal, and yard upkeep. Many, if not all, of these expenses will rise each year.

Total Debt Load

An investor who borrows funds to finance the purchase of a property must know how much the payments of loan and principal will be for the year.

If the loan is in the form of a fixed mortgage, the figure will remain steady. With an adjustable rate mortgage, the interest may rise or fall after a set number of months. With a balloon mortgage, there is a set term of years of interest-only payments at either a fixed rate or an adjustable rate, with the entire balance of the loan due at the end of that term.

Let us figure out the annual cash flow on a fictional duplex that a husband and wife purchased as ABC, LLC, a limited liability company. Assume that the asking price for the property was $130,000 and that ABC succeeded in negotiating the price down 10 percent to $117,000. The two units in the duplex bring in a total of $1,200 per month, or $14,400 per year.

Let us further assume the following annual operating expenses:

Property taxes	$2,000
Insurance	$1,400
Maintenance/repairs	$1,000
Sewer charges	$250
Misc. gov't fees	$100
ANNUAL EXPENSES	**$4,750**

Also assume that ABC paid a 10 percent down payment, or $11,700, and financed the rest of the purchase price, $105,300, at a 6 percent interest rate for 30 years. (You can easily find mortgage calculators by searching the Web.)

$105,300 x 6 percent interest amortized over 30 years = $631.33 per month

$631.33 x 12 months = $7,576 per year in mortgage payments

Next add the annual expenses and the total debt service on the loan:

Annual expenses	$4,750
Annual mortgage payments	$7,576
TOTAL ANNUAL COST	**$12,326**

For the final part of the cash flow calculation, subtract the total annual cost from the total annual gross income.

Annual gross income (rents)	$14,400
Total annual cost	-12,326
ANNUAL CASH FLOW	**$2,074**

The calculation reveals a positive annual cash flow of $2,074 per year, or $172.83 per month. After all that math, that may seem like a small amount of money to pocket.

Let us continue the math a little longer so that we can calculate the rate of return on the cash that ABC laid out to get the property: the $11,700 down payment. We do this by dividing the annual cash flow by the down payment:

$2,074 (annual cash flow) ÷ $11,700 (down payment) = 17.73%

That $2,074 cash flow does not seem so small when we figure out that it represents almost an 18 percent return on ABC's cash outlay. Try finding that rate of return on other types of investments (not counting highly risky vehicles, such as "junk" bonds).

When doing these calculations, bear in mind that annual expenses change every year due to tax increases and other rising costs or unexpected expenditures. By the same token, the rents you charge for your properties also should go up each year. Yet, you might also have one or more vacancies during the year, which will affect the gross annual income. For these reasons, it is wise to recalculate these figures each year to see whether expenses can be trimmed or whether some other adjustment is possible to protect your ROI. See Chapter 19 for a more detailed examination of how to properly handle these expenses.

Appreciation

When a property appreciates, its value has increased, and the property can command a higher sale price. This, in turn, increases the owner's equity in the property, normally with no effort on his or her part. (Equity is the amount of real estate that is owned free and clear of debt.) The two main drivers of appreciation are inflation and demand. Appreciation also can often be forced.

Inflation

Simply put, when prices go up, appreciation occurs. The price of property, like the price of food, fuel, and cars, can be driven up by factors such as the rate of inflation of the national economy or deficit spending by the government. When the U.S. inflation rate rises, the appreciation rate of property rises as well, making it cost more, even if it is not worth more. Appreciation builds an owner's profit potential in property.

Inflation affects the price of land and the price of the structures that are on it in different ways. This is because land does not wear out, but structures deteriorate over time. It is the value of the land, rather than the value of its structures, that has the greatest effect on the increase in value from inflation. This is known as the land-to-improvement ratio.

The land-to-improvement ratio can vary widely from one area of the country to another or even from one neighborhood of a city to another. The value of land in urban areas can be up to 90 percent of the value of the entire piece of property, with the structures on it representing only 10 percent of the value. In contrast, in some rural areas, a structure might represent 90 percent of a property's value, and the land may be only 10 percent.

Demand Appreciation

Demand is another factor that can push up the price of real estate. The main economic principles that affect demand appreciation are scarcity, transferability, utility, and demand. In combination, these principles work to drive up the value of property at a greater rate in some areas and to push down value in others.

Scarcity

A desirable commodity that is in short supply commands higher prices. In real estate, the greatest demand appreciation occurs in densely populated metropolitan areas because there is little or no land for expansion and new construction. Often, the only way to make land available is to knock down older buildings, warehouses, and other structures that are on the land. A developer that finds a property owner who is willing to sell must pay for the land and the structures on it. This makes the property more expensive for a developer. In contrast, the greater availability of vacant land in rural areas often means that a developer can pay lower prices.

Transferability

Also known as "liquidity," the ease with which commodities can be bought and sold affects the demand for those commodities. Investments such as stocks and bonds are fairly liquid in the sense that they can be transferred readily from one owner to another. Real estate is not as liquid because it cannot be transferred as quickly. The inherent structure of the process of buying and selling real estate, the limited pool of potential buyers, and the difficulties of interested buyers in obtaining adequate financing all inhibit the transferability of real estate.

Utility

The greater the usefulness of a property, the greater the value of the property can be. "Highest and best use" is a concept in real estate that recognizes that a property may yield more profit from other uses than it does from its current use. Some examples of highest and best use that may not be obvious include a house sitting on a double lot that can be subdivided, a residential building on a commercial lot near a rapidly developing area, and a house or a unit that has sufficient space that can be easily converted into an additional bedroom (with a corresponding increase in rental value).

Demand

The more desirable an item is, the greater is its value. When stocks are hot, their prices shoot up. When stocks are falling and bond yields rise, investors sell their stocks and park their money in bonds; it is the same with real estate. When properties start moving and investors notice, more people want to buy. This increased demand for a limited supply of property drives up the appreciation rate of real estate. In some areas, demand — and the corresponding price of property — can vary from block to block.

Demand can be driven up in another way. Because the price of investment real estate is directly related to the net income that the property generates, an increase in a property's income stream can increase the value of the property, even if the demand from investors has not increased. In such a situation, the demand comes from the willingness of tenants to pay more rent for a property, such as when there are many tenants in an area but a limited supply of units to rent.

Forced Appreciation

An investor can force the appreciation of his or her property by doing something to the property that increases its value. This can be anything from fixing a run-down house to replacing bad management with good management to improving rent collections. Some experts believe that forced appreciation is the road to the biggest profits and the fastest accumulation of wealth. See more on this later, in Chapter 9.

Equity Growth Through Loan Reduction

A proactive way to make the equity in a property grow is by paying down the loan used to buy the property. Understand that the amount of the down payment represents the initial equity owned in a property. If you, the investor, use no loans and instead pay cash for a property, you start with 100 percent equity.

In contrast, if an investor pays a 5 percent down payment and finances the other 95 percent, he or she starts with 5 percent equity in the property. The monthly mortgage payments consist of a portion for principal and a portion for interest. As the investor makes the monthly mortgage payments, the equity grows with each portion of the principal included in those payments. (This assumes that the investor did not overpay for the property and that market conditions are such that the price of the property does not decrease). In the beginning, a large portion of the monthly mortgage payment goes toward interest, but over the years, a greater portion goes toward reducing the principal amount of the loan, which in turn leads to a quicker buildup of equity.

Tax Benefits

The U.S. tax code provides real estate investors with several tax breaks. One break stems from the deduction of costs involved in making the purchase. Another break is in the form of depreciation, which is effectively a paper loss that can be deducted from the taxable income received from a property. Yet another break comes from the deduction of operating expenses incurred in connection with the property.

A wise investor will use the services of an accountant, a tax attorney, or some other tax advisor, because the tax laws and rules are complicated and always changing. Nevertheless, to properly evaluate the potential of a piece of property, the investor should have a working understanding of the basic tax principles at play.

Purchase Expenses

Broadly speaking, an investor can deduct most of the expenses incurred when he or she bought the property. This tax deduction must be taken for the year in which the purchase occurred. The deductible purchase expenses include:

- Liability and fire insurance

- Interest prepaid on the loan

- Escrow fees

- Title insurance

- Prorated property taxes

- Attorney fees

- Various lender fees

Loan fees, or "points," are treated differently. They fall in the category of funds paid to obtain a new loan and, as such, must be written off over the life of the loan. To see how this plays out, assume that a bank will give you a 30-year $150,000 mortgage and that it charges a loan fee of 1.25 percent. This is how you calculate the yearly deduction:

Step one: $150,000 (loan amount) x 1.25 percent (loan fee rate) = $1,875 (loan fee)

Step two: $1,875 (loan fee) ÷ 30 years (loan term) = $62.50 deductible per year

This means that you would be entitled to deduct $62.50 per year for 30 years for the points charged to you by the bank for the mortgage.

Depreciation

The structures on a piece of property deteriorate over time. Under the U.S. tax code, the owner of investment property may take an annual depreciation allowance against his or her income. The theory behind this allowance is that the owner will use the savings from the deduction to replace the deteriorated structure at the end of its useful life. Although the theory may play out in other types of businesses that use equipment that wears out quickly, owners of investment real estate rarely hold on to properties so long that the structures on them wear out. As a result, the tax savings from the annual depreciation allowance works as a profit for the property owner.

There are several alternative ways to determine the annual depreciation allowance for tax purposes. You need to consult your accountant or tax advisor about which alternative is best for your particular situation.

One way to get a rough calculation of depreciation is by using information from the tax bill for the property. The tax bill identifies the assessed value of improvements, which are the structures on the land, and the total assessed value of the entire property. The dollar amounts on the tax bill may not reflect the true market value of the property, but this is not important. What matters is the following equation:

assessed improvement value ÷ total assessed value = % value of improvements

The next step is to take the percentage of the value of improvements to determine the amount of depreciable improvements:

% value of improvements x price of property = depreciable improvements

This way of determining depreciation from tax bill information may not raise a red flag at the IRS, but the ratio may not be accurate.

Another way to determine depreciation is by using the appraisal that was performed when the investor bought the property. The appraiser's opinion about the value of land and the improvements can be found in the section of the appraisal on the reproduction cost method. The reproduction cost is the appraiser's estimate of the cost to build the improvements as of the date of the appraisal. An allowance is made for depreciation, and the rest is the appraiser's value of the improvements. You then calculate as follows:

Step one: estimated value of improvements ÷ appraised value = % value of improvements

Step two: % value of improvements x price = depreciable improvements

Under IRS rules, you must stick with the depreciation method that you select when you put your property "in service" until you have used up all the depreciation write-off. You have the time between the closing of title to the deadline of your tax return to select a depreciation method.

The next step for determining the percentage return from tax benefits entails applying the Modified Accelerated Cost Recovery System (MACRS), which establishes the useful life, or "recovery period," for the depreciation of assets under the U.S. tax code. For real estate with structures, the recovery period is 27.5 years for residential property and 39 years for nonresidential commercial property.

This is how to figure out the annual depreciation allowance using the MACRS:

Value of depreciable improvements ÷ recovery period = annual depreciation allowance

Operating Expenses

The expenses incurred to operate a property are deductible, although the IRS distinguishes "expense items" from "capital items."

Expense Items

The rule is that the expenses incurred to fix problems at a building or to maintain the value of the property are the normal operating expenses that are deductible in the year that they were paid. Examples of expense items include:

- Interest on loans

- Insurance

- Property taxes

- License and municipal fees

- Utilities

- Cleaning expenses

- Lawn/gardening expenses

- Plumbing, electrical, roofing, and other repairs

- Management fees

- Advertising fees

- Rental commissions

- Mileage, telephone, and postal expenses

Capital Items

Capital items comprise improvements that increase the value of property or completely replace a component of the property. These costs must be depreciated over time instead of being deducted in full for the year in which they are incurred. The U.S. tax code recognizes capital improvements that add value to the asset (the property) or significantly increase the time that the asset can be used. Capital items must be written off over the period of time that they contribute to the property's usefulness. Examples of capital items include:

- New roof

- New electrical wiring

- New plumbing

- Carpets or drapes

- Building additions

- Major appliances

- Major repairs, such as new siding or a new driveway

- New flooring

State Income Taxes as an Additional Boon

Although many states have their own income tax rates, their rules mimic the federal rules on deductions and depreciation. An investor who lives in a state with an income tax will see additional savings. The formula under the MACRS can be used to calculate the state savings.

Other Tax Considerations

There are many other tax considerations that apply to the different phases of ownership. For example, some tax rules for "active" investors are different from those for "passive" investors. These categories are determined by the amount of involvement that the investor has in the management of a property.

There are also limitations on the use of losses from real estate against earnings from an individual's primary profession.

In addition, when contemplating the sale of property, an investor will have to deal with capital gains taxes, which are taxes on the profits made from the sale.

One way to deal with the capital gains tax is the 1031 tax-deferred exchange, named after the section of the U.S. tax code in which it is discussed. A 1031 exchange allows an investor to use the taxes owed on the capital gains from the sale of one property as a down payment on the purchase of another property of the same kind and of equal or greater value. In terms of investment properties, the idea behind this type of exchange is that one income-producing property is being exchanged for another. Therefore, an investment triplex cannot be traded for a new residence for the buyer, but the triplex can be traded for a commercial property, such as one with an office building on it. There are different categories of 1031 exchanges, each with their own set of definitions and rules. An investor should consult his or her accountant or tax professional for a detailed explanation of 1031 exchanges.

An installment sale is another way to defer capital gains taxes. In this type of scenario, the seller also functions as one of the lenders, or even as the sole lender, for the purchaser. The seller pays the capital gains tax only on the portion of profit received each year from the installment payments made by the buyer. Not only does the seller earn interest on capital gains that are being deferred, he or she also can get a higher interest rate by carrying the buyer's financing than by putting the money in a bank or some other "safe" investment.

3

PROTECT YOUR PERSONAL ASSETS

One of the main reasons often cited for the failure of many people to invest in residential real estate is the reluctance to deal with tenants and property-management issues. With enough information and experience, this reluctance can be overcome, as will be seen in Part III. Yet, a more disturbing threat lurks beneath the relationship that an owner has with his or her tenants and properties: the loss of personal assets, such as cash and home, in the event of a lawsuit or other legal claim.

The worst-case scenario is along the lines of a tenant and his or her family being injured by a roof collapse and then taking the owner to court on a personal injury claim. Assuming that the company that insures the building would have a legitimate reason not to pay the claim, an owner who fails to take steps to protect his or her personal assets before becoming a landlord could be facing a nightmare.

If an investor instead chooses an appropriate legal form in which to own residential properties, such as duplexes, triplexes, fourplexes, and mobile homes, he or she can put his or her personal assets beyond the reach of others.

The following is a brief examination of various ways in which real estate can be owned. It is not an exhaustive list, and a legal advisor should be consulted to determine which form of ownership is best, given an investor's particular situation, needs, and goals.

Choose the Right Entity

Sole Proprietorship

The simplest way to get into real estate investment is to buy property in one's own name. The name of the owner would go on the deed to the property, all applicable government records, the mortgage documents, and the insurance policy. On the other hand, because other people and entities — tenants, the lender, and even the IRS — will be involved in this venture in one form or another, a sole proprietorship is not the safe way to go, even if the owner has few personal assets. In the sole proprietor form of ownership, the owner is liable for claims against him or her, even if they relate to an investment property. This means that the owner cannot shield his or her personal assets, such as bank accounts or even his or her own home. This is also true if a married couple or other individuals buy a property together in their own names.

General Partnership

A general partnership is a legal entity in which two or more people come together to invest in a business or other venture under certain terms set out in a partnership agreement. All the members are general partners, meaning that they all have a say in the management of the partnership's affairs. It also means that all the partners are liable for the debts and liabilities of the partnership. The partnership itself is not taxed, and the taxable income and losses pass through to the partners, who must pay their pro rata share of taxes that are due. A partnership ceases to exist when it is dissolved, the partners all die, or only one person is left.

Limited Partnership

In this form of ownership, there is at least one general partner and one or more limited partners. The general partner has the authority to find, negotiate for, and buy properties in the name of the limited partnership, and he or she also handles the day-to-day management of the partnership and its assets. In addition, the general partner has unlimited liability for the activities of the partnership. In contrast, the limited partners have no management duties, and their liability for partnership activities is limited to the amount of their investment. Limited partners are sometimes referred to as "silent" partners. The taxation is handled in the same manner as that of a general partnership.

C Corporation

A C corporation is a highly formal entity with a life of its own. To start a C corporation, its founders must file articles of incorporation, more often than not in their home state, although the founders may determine that it is more beneficial to be incorporated in another state. Shares in the corporation must be issued, a board of directors must be appointed, officers must be selected, and an annual meeting at which minutes are kept must be held. Under a C corporation, the owners are almost entirely immune from personal liability. Unlike a partnership, a C corporation continues to exist even if its owners die or leave.

Regarding real estate, there are several downsides to the C corporation form of ownership. In several jurisdictions, corporate officers or directors may be held criminally liable if the corporation fails to correct building-code violations at properties owned in the corporate name. C corporations must pay taxes on the capital gains generated when properties are sold; if the remaining amount is distributed to the shareholders as dividends or to the officers as salary, the recipients of those distributions must pay taxes on the amount received. This double taxation makes a C corporation a questionable entity for the ownership of investment real estate. Yet another downside is the fact that it is complicated to terminate a C corporation.

S Corporation

An S corporation requires the same formalities and provides the same type of shield from personal liability as does a C corporation. The main difference is how S corporations are treated under the U.S. tax code. There is no double taxation because the tax liability generated by an S corporation passes through to its shareholders; this is why S corporations are also known as "pass-through tax entities." Nonetheless, the losses that pass through to a shareholder ordinarily cannot exceed the amount of the shareholder's investment. Unlike a C corporation, an S corporation cannot have more than 75 shareholders, shareholders who are not U.S. citizens, or more than one class of stock.

Limited Liability Company

A limited liability company normally provides the same shield from personal liability that is available through a corporation. Like an S corporation, a limited liability company is a pass-through tax entity, which eliminates the problem of double taxation. It is also simpler and less expensive to set up than a corporation and does not require formalities, such as annual meetings. A limited liability company can even consist of just one person, who can report the company's taxable activities on his or her individual tax return. For these reasons, many investors in real estate prefer this form of ownership.

Limited Liability Partnership

A limited liability partnership functions like a hybrid of a corporation and a partnership. The partners are fully or partially shielded personally for the liabilities, debts, and other obligations of the partnership, and all profits and losses pass through to the partners. The limited liability partnership itself is not taxed. Not all states recognize this entity, so check your state's statutes to determine whether forming a limited liability partnership is possible and, if so, the extent of a partner's personal liability.

Advanced Asset Protection

There are many other ways to protect assets. These methods include having separate limited liability companies for the purchase of different properties, using multiple entities, forming family limited partnerships and family savings trusts, and engaging in equity stripping with an equity reduction plan. Not all jurisdictions will recognize all these methods. Investors should consult their attorneys and tax advisers for more information.

CASE STUDY: RICHARD SELTZER, ESQ.

436 Central Ave.
Jersey City, NJ 07307
(201) 795-9695
Richard@Seltzer-law.com

I am a general practitioner with more than 30 years of experience representing clients in real estate and business transactions. I have been investing in rental properties since 1982. I have owned many two- to four-family homes, and some of the ground floors in several of my buildings have been storefronts.

In my little game, I was getting three fees: as an investor, a lawyer, and a manager. I convinced my friends from Manhattan to invest with me by promising them that I would be responsible for the management and going to court, and they had no problem paying me. In the beginning, before the invention of the limited liability company, we formed limited partnerships to buy the properties. Another fee I used to get was the general partner fee for being the one who signed the mortgages and notes. When the limited liability companies came along in the early 1990s, we could get the benefit of a partnership with the insulation of the liabilities of a corporation all at the same time.

If I had known better when I started out, I would have had fewer partners and put more of my own money into the investments. Instead, the comfort level I needed at that time required that I have many partnerships and many partners. For example, if I had $50,000, I would put $10,000 into five deals with several partners rather than have two deals and put $25,000 in each. Only in the past five or seven years have I started being a little more aggressive and less risk-adverse.

My advice for people interested investing in rental properties is: (1) don't think you are going into a glamorous business; it is mundane with no sex appeal, (2) don't be greedy, and (3) don't go into too much debt.

4

ASSEMBLE YOUR TEAM OF EXPERTS

By this point, you may be thinking that there is much information to absorb, substantial research to undertake, and too many accounting and legal nuances to grasp.

One of the advantages of investing in real estate is that you do not have to be an expert in all its aspects. You do not have to — and should not — jump into residential multiunit or mobile-home investing and try to figure everything out by yourself. You will have a much greater chance of success if you put together a team of at least the following professionals:

- Real estate agent or broker

- Real estate attorney

- Accountant, tax attorney, or other tax advisor

- Insurance agent

A smart investor will put a team together before he or she zeros in on a property. By having a team of professionals in place, the investor will have advisors to help him or her determine what to look for in a property and, therefore, which properties are worthy of offers. With a team in place, the investor also will be ready to close titles more quickly, smoothly, and confidently when the right deal comes along than would be possible if he or she had to start looking for experts after an offer was accepted.

How a Real Estate Agent is Key

A real estate broker or agent who is experienced in investment-property transactions is the linchpin of a real estate investor's team. The difference between a broker and an agent is that the broker has passed more tests to obtain a state license as a broker. The broker is ultimately responsible for the actions of the agents who report to him or her. Because brokers and agents are equally qualified to handle real estate listings and transactions, for the sake of brevity, all subsequent referrals to "real estate agents" will encompass real estate brokers.

It is important for an investor to find and work with a real estate agent who is experienced, professional in manner, and knowledgeable about the area targeted by the investor. Another important characteristic is compatibility with the investor. After all, as the investor builds a portfolio of properties along with his or her wealth, the investor will have many dealings with the agent, who has a vested interest in helping the investor reach his or her goals. Such a symbiotic relationship must be built on mutual trust, respect, and understanding. Moreover, a seasoned real estate agent can be valuable to a novice investor. Some experts also recommend that an agent have experience as an investor.

There are various ways of finding a real estate agent. "For Sale" signs on properties that are listed through real estate agencies include the name and contact information of the listing agent; this will require cold-calling an agent and then gauging his or her abilities and personality. A better way to find an agent is through other investors in multiunit residential properties who should be able to recommend good agents they have used or encountered. Alternatively, an investor can ask an agent that he or she has used in one region for the name of agents in other regions; the investor also can ask his or her lawyer or local property management companies for the names of real estate agents with whom they are familiar.

Although it may seem easier to look at property listings in newspapers or the Web, Internet or newspaper listings normally include only how many bedrooms and bathrooms a property has, whereas an agent has access to much more information. According to Stephen DiClemente, a licensed real estate agent with Re/Max Tri County in Hamilton, New Jersey, an agent can tell an investor about the rents and expenses at a property. "If we do not have an answer, we can go to the listing agent, who can contact the owner for the information," said DiClemente.

When an investor contacts a real estate agent about purchasing property, the agent initially will go through all the properties that are currently on the market to find the ones that match what the investor wants. As the agent begins to show properties and to know the investor better, the agent will get a better idea of the features in a property that the investor seeks and of the type of property that is suitable to the investor's needs and available financing.

Yet, there is no substitute for an investor doing his or her own homework. Because real estate agents are legally bound to be impartial, they are not permitted to say anything about neighborhoods, such as about the incidence of crime or whether a particular area is "up and coming." As DiClemente explained, "I can [only] show you what other homes in the neighborhood sold for, what the rents are in a neighborhood, anything that has to do with the real estate." An agent also can tell an investor where to go, such as to the local police department or certain Web sites to find crime statistics for particular neighborhoods.

It is important to distinguish a listing, or seller's, agent from a buyer's agent. The listing agent represents the seller and is responsible for marketing the property. The seller and the listing agent sign a listing agreement that sets out the price and terms sought by the seller, size of the lot, number of units, income generated, annual property taxes, and other data. Most properties that are for sale are entered into the local Multiple Listing Service (MLS), to which all other agents have access. The listing agreement also includes the percentage of the sales price that will be the commission; the listing agent is by and large entitled to one-half of that commission plus an additional sum of about $50. The seller is responsible for paying the commission, but the commission is frequently factored into the price of the property.

In contrast, a buyer's agent works for the purchaser and is the one to present the purchaser's offer to the listing agent. The buyer's agent is entitled to the remaining one-half of the commission.

Sometimes the same agent, or two agents in the same real estate agency, will be responsible for listing a property and obtaining a buyer for it. In that case, a dual agency relationship is created and must be disclosed to the buyer. The buyer then is asked to sign a form in which he or she consents to the dual agency. A dual agency relationship often works out fine, but there can be times when the conflicting interests of the seller and the buyer put the agent in a bind. If an investor is uncomfortable with a dual agency relationship and is concerned that his or her interests could be compromised, he or she may have to walk away from a property and find another that does not raise dual agency issues.

Although the involvement of real estate agents will mean higher costs in a real estate transaction, good agents are worth the extra expense because they can help uncover properties that could escape the attention of an investor who relies on his or her own efforts. DiClemente points out that even after a purchase has been completed, an agent can continue to alert an investor of additional properties that come on the market if the investor has expressed an interest in making more purchases. Successful investors also know that a competent agent is an excellent source of information on current real estate market conditions. Finally, an agent with proven marketing skills will be essential when the investor decides to sell his or her properties.

How a Real Estate Attorney Watches Your Back

In a real estate or mobile home transaction, a lawyer regularly does not enter the picture until after a seller and a buyer have signed a contract. In some states, the parties to a real estate contract have several days to have the contract reviewed by their respective lawyers. Even in places where such attorney review periods are not the usual practice, it is a good idea to include an attorney-review contingency clause in the contract. This simply means that the contract should include a paragraph that recognizes the parties' right to have the contract reviewed by their respective attorneys and that makes the offer contingent on the review and final approval of the contract by the attorneys.

Nonetheless, this does not mean that an investor should wait until the start of the attorney-review period to line up a lawyer. As part of the preparation process, an investor should ask other investors, real estate agents, or an attorney whom he or she has used in non-real estate matters for the names of lawyers experienced in real estate. An experienced real estate lawyer is an essential, valuable member of a real estate investor's team of experts.

Even if the investor lives in a jurisdiction that allows closings without the assistance of lawyers, the smart investor should not be tempted to save time and money by forgoing such assistance. Estelle Flynn Lord, an attorney in Westfield, New Jersey, with 24 years of experience in the purchase and sale of real estate and mobile homes, calls such a move "penny-wise and pound-foolish." Even if a transaction appears to be easy, a buyer should be represented by an attorney because, as Flynn Lord noted, "It is often the deals which seem the simplest that turn out to be the real nightmares."

Attorneys such as Lord believe that it is more prudent if a buyer involves the attorney early in the process. An investor often needs to have certain contract clauses explained thoroughly by a lawyer before signing the contract. Additionally, an investor is not likely to know the intricacies of the law of real property, the roots of which date back to feudal times. As Lord advised, "An investor should find an attorney who is experienced in residential and commercial properties, because this way, the attorney has a full spectrum of knowledge on which to draw and can better anticipate the potential expensive pitfalls that await the buyer." In short, an experienced lawyer can save the investor time by answering questions promptly and money by insisting on the inclusion of certain terms in the contract that protect the investor's interests, such as mortgage and property-inspection contingency clauses.

An investor also can take comfort in the fact that the attorney works solely on the investor's behalf. "Unlike a real estate agent or a mortgage lender, an attorney will not have a hidden agenda or interest in having a deal go through even if the terms of the sale are unfavorable to the investor," observed Flynn Lord.

In particular, a lawyer will prove valuable to an investor if, among other things:

- The contract contains terms that are not readily understood

- The preprinted contract does not cover the particular situation of the parties

- The property includes complex leases

- Complex financing will be involved

- There are potential problems with the title

- There are potential problems with hidden conditions at the property, such as the presence of hazardous substances or underground oil tanks

After an investor has used the services of a good lawyer for one or more transactions, he or she will likely find that the lawyer does not mind answering questions that come up during negotiations for other properties. The lawyer can advise the investor on what points to press, what points to avoid, and what issues are problematic under the law. A lawyer can also keep an investor on track when doing due diligence, which we will examine in Chapter 8.

An investor in multiunit residential property also must remember that he or she will have to abide by the landlord/tenant laws of the state in which the property is located and the landlord/tenant ordinances of the local municipality and should speak with the attorney about this. The information obtained may affect the investor's decision about the maximum number of units that should be in a building that he or she would consider buying and whether to hire a management company to handle tenancy matters.

How a Tax Advisor Can Keep Money in Your Pocket

A certified public accountant, tax attorney, or other tax professional who has experience with real estate investors can provide valuable information about the types of investments that suit an individual's particular financial abilities, needs, and goals. (These pros will be referred to here as "tax advisors.") The tax advisor must also have experience with the tax laws of the jurisdiction in which the property is located.

There are many ways in which a good tax advisor can help an investor's bottom line. Even before approaching a real estate agent, an investor should consider seeking out the services of a tax advisor. The advisor can recommend specific tax strategies and can open the investor's eyes to tax benefits — and dangers — that are not self-evident. After the purchase of a property, the advisor can inform the investor of how involved to be in the management of a property to meet the active-participation requirement of some tax laws, even if a property management company has been hired. When the time comes to sell a property, the advisor can recommend legitimate ways to reduce or defer the capital gains taxes from the sale.

These are just a few examples of how a tax advisor earns a place on a real estate investor's team. The tax laws are extremely complex, and understanding them and their interplay is beyond the ability of most non-tax professionals. Therefore, an individual should not hesitate to get the help that is essential for succeeding in the property-investment game.

How an Insurance Agent Can Help You Focus and Leverage

An often overlooked element of determining ROI is the cost of premiums for fire and liability insurance on a property. An experienced, independent insurance agent (meaning one who is not tied to any one insurance company) can tell you what is and is not an insurable risk and about the range of premiums charged by insurers in a given area. This information can save an investor an enormous amount of time because it alerts him or her about geographic areas in which the insurance would be prohibitively expensive.

An insurance agent also can advise an investor about telltale signs of trouble from the insurer's point of view, such as boarded-up homes in the vicinity of the property being considered or a string of "For Sale" signs up and down the street; to an insurer, this may signal that an area is going downhill and losing value. The insurance agent also can tell an investor what facts to obtain about a property, such as the age of the roof, heating system, and hot-water heater and when the electrical and plumbing systems were last updated; this information can provide the investor with leverage when negotiating with the seller. In addition, the agent can help the investor obtain flood insurance if the property is located in a flood zone.

An investor almost certainly would not have to look far to find a good insurance agent. He or she can start with the agent who already knows him or her and who has handled his or her personal insurance needs. If that agent cannot provide the type of service required by the investor, the agent can recommend others who can.

Basic coverage under an insurance policy for a nonowner-occupied rental property protects the real estate investor from losses from fires, windstorms, burglaries, vandalism, and even civil unrest, to name a few conditions. Liability insurance is part of a comprehensive policy, and it covers injuries to others or losses suffered by them as a result of dangerous or defective conditions on a property as well as the legal costs of defending oneself in a personal injury lawsuit. An insurance agent can explain exactly what is and is not covered. The agent will likely suggest other types of coverage, such as for loss of rent when a property becomes uninhabitable due to damage from a fire or other disaster. With the assistance of the insurance agent, the investor can determine a comfortable level of deductibles and also which types of coverage are not necessary for the location and type of property involved.

Optional Members of the Team

A mortgage broker or lender, an appraiser, and a property inspector are other professionals who could round out a real estate investor's team. The same is true of the skilled professionals at a title insurance company. The reasons that these pros were not included as part of the core team are covered in the following descriptions.

Mortgage Broker/Lender

A mortgage broker is a person or firm that represents several mortgage lenders and that arranges financing for borrowers who are buying real estate. The lender or borrower pays the broker a fee when the loan closes. Good mortgage brokers can help a borrower find financing from unusual sources or through little-known programs.

An investor who wants to strike up a relationship with a mortgage broker or lender should look for one (or more) who understands real estate market cycles and is experienced in the type of properties that the investor seeks in the targeted area. By providing a mortgage broker or lender with truthful information about his or her finances, the investor can find out before even looking at properties how much of a down payment he or she will need to make and how much he or she can expect to borrow. These figures are an indispensable part of an investor's calculations. Moreover, being pre-approved for a mortgage will save time and provide a valuable bargaining chip during the search for properties.

Some real estate investment experts advise investors to cultivate relationships with mortgage brokers or lenders, even if it means paying a slightly higher interest rate on a loan. Yet, an investor should not lose sight of the fact that mortgage brokers and lenders are in business to make money. An investor must always keep an eye on his or her bottom line and search out the best loan terms possible.

Another point to consider is that while mortgage brokers and lenders apply certain criteria and decide the maximum amount that an investor is qualified to borrow, they are not the ones who should determine whether the investor should borrow up to that maximum. Only the investor should decide how much he or she can comfortably borrow in accordance to his or her financial projections for a given property. This is one of the key ways in which an investor controls the degree of risk that he or she will take.

Title Insurance Company

A title insurance company (also called "title company" and "title insurer") searches the county records to uncover outstanding liens on a property. If liens turn up, the investor or the investor's attorney must find out whether the liens were paid off but never removed from the books. A title company also checks for any open judgments against people or entities with names that are the same as or similar to those of the sellers. The presence of easements and other interests in a property that are not obvious can also be revealed by a good title search. Then, for a one-time fee, a title company insures the title for the benefit of the buyer.

For investors who go on to buy more properties, it may be worthwhile to use the same title company for each transaction. After the title company gets to know the investor and realizes that there is the possibility of additional title insurance premiums, it will be more willing to help the investor sort out title problems that may turn up.

On the other hand, an investor's attorney may prefer to use a title company other than the one that an investor likes. Assuming that the attorney does not have a personal interest in his or her preferred title company, it would be up to the investor and the attorney to work out which title insurer to use.

Property Inspector

Unless a real estate investor is an experienced contractor or builder, he or she needs the services of a professional property inspector. A diligent, competent property inspector is valuable. The inspector can confirm to the investor that the property being considered is in acceptable condition or can uncover serious structural defects and other physical problems at the property that would be costly to fix. If the investor determines that the property is worth buying despite its problems, he or she may be able to use the defects found by the property inspector as leverage to obtain a price reduction or other concessions from the seller.

A property inspector is qualified to evaluate the many components of a building, including the roof; electrical, plumbing, and heating systems; and the structural foundation. A thorough property inspection pays for itself when it uncovers items that must be repaired by the seller at a cost that exceeds that of the inspection. As the property inspector goes through a building with the buyer, the inspector can point out other items that will need repair or replacement in the future and what that will cost.

Although an investor might want to rely on only one property inspector for all the properties considered, the inspector may not want or be able to visit properties outside his or her territory.

Appraiser

An investor who buys property with his or her own funds or with financing from other private sources should hire an appraiser to ascertain the value of the property. The appraiser can inform the investor about the value of the property in its current condition and its projected value after repairs and upgrades, as well as what it will cost for the repairs and upgrades. Armed with this information and the figures from comparable sales in the target area, the investor can make an informed decision about the highest price that he or she is prepared to pay for a property.

An appraiser whose services are used routinely by an investor also is able to inform him or her about distressed properties that have much hidden potential. In other words, the appraiser will know which properties in good areas have been neglected and can be bought for a reasonable price because they require work.

A number of real estate investment experts believe that an appraiser is a valuable member of an investor's team. This becomes irrelevant when conventional lenders, such as banks and mortgage lenders, will be providing the financing. Those lenders have their own appraisers on whom they rely, and the borrower has little say in the choice of appraiser.

CASE STUDY: ESTELLE FLYNN LORD, ESQ.

111 Quimby St.
Westfield, NJ 07090
(908) 654-3883
Estelle.Lord@verizon.net

In my 24 years of practicing law, I have represented numerous clients in the purchase and sale of single- and multifamily houses and mobile homes.

A novice investor should contact an experienced real estate attorney early in the process. The attorney can go over how to assemble a team of experts and what to expect at each step leading to the closing, including contract negotiations.

I think many people have been facing foreclosure because they did not take out their calculators and do the math for themselves. Often, inexperienced investors fail to factor in the property taxes, interest, insurance at commercial rates, and other items.

Investors need to be aware that if they will not be living on the property, a conventional lender will try to put them in the commercial loan market, where the interest rates are higher than for residential properties.

Even with all the potential pitfalls, I believe that real estate is the best investment around. Each time your tenants pay rent that goes toward the mortgage, your equity in the property increases. Over time, the value of the property also increases. Now that prices are coming down, it is a good time to jump in if you have some guts and understand what you are doing. Buy low now and you will end up with a good, secure investment when prices go up again in the next few years.

My advice to people interested in investing in rental property is: (1) consult a real estate attorney before you put a bid on a property, (2) have a professional property inspection, (3) don't be afraid to ask "stupid" questions when you are making your calculations, (4) be aware of what the local tenancy laws say, and (5) do your due diligence.

5

MAKE A PLAN

This chapter reveals how to come up with a plan for investing in multiunit residential properties. Many of these pointers apply equally to a plan for investing in mobile homes.

It is important to have an investment plan. As previously mentioned, investing in real estate must be treated as a business. For the investor, the investment plan is the business plan. Other types of businesses rarely thrive if they are started without a decent business plan.

A real estate investment plan is a road map. If you tried driving from Miami to San Francisco without a map, you would know that you have to head west. Nonetheless, unless you know how to navigate by the sun and the stars, you most likely would not know which roads to take. You would waste gasoline, money, and time by not consulting a map. The same is true if you invest in real estate without a plan. You need to know what to buy, where to buy, how much to spend, and when to sell.

This chapter could also be called "Due Diligence in the Pre-Search Phase" because it describes the steps that a serious investor must take before looking at properties to:

- Determine financial goals, a schedule for achieving those goals, and what properties will need to return to help meet those goals

- Calculate different financial scenarios to achieve those goals — including different potential down-payment amounts, the corresponding amounts that would need to be financed, intelligent estimates of the operating expenses of properties, and the amount of rental income needed to cover all the relevant expenses

- Understand what types of property to seek based on those calculations

In other words, this is the most important phase for anyone who wants to invest successfully in multiunit residential properties, mobile homes, and mobile-home parks. Setting your goals down on paper in an orderly fashion may seem intimidating or tedious, but there is no better way of removing the elements of fear and unbridled risk that often stop a would-be real estate investor in his or her tracks.

Grab a pencil, some paper, and a calculator, and let the numbers help you cast away your doubts.

Determine Your Financial Goals

The starting point is determining why you want to invest in residential property. Ask yourself what you hope to accomplish, what your financial goals are, and what your schedule is for accomplishing those goals.

Perhaps you have a satisfactory career and merely need a little side business to offset your income taxes. In that case, it may be enough for you to find a duplex with rents that will provide a small amount of cash flow and a fair amount of deductible expenses.

On the other hand, you may have a job you want to leave or that does not pay you enough. You might be concerned about being downsized. Getting a steady flow of income from a secondary source will give you a sense of security. A few mobile homes or a small residential property with low expenses and good cash flow could be your ticket to peace of mind in such a situation.

Maybe you want to build your net worth over time. You decide what that time period should be — five, ten, or fifteen years. Then you can see whether your best strategy is to buy several properties, flip some to generate cash to buy some more, and hold on to the rest as the equity builds through inflation, appreciation, and debt pay down.

Your Cash Flow Needs

You need to determine whether you want to pull out a significant amount of cash regularly from the property or you do not need the cash right now.

How much cash you use initially in the purchase of a property and how you manage the debt and operational expenses after you buy the property will affect the cash flow. Thus, the bigger the down payment on a property, the smaller the mortgage payments will be. This means that less of the monthly rental payment will be eaten up by the debt pay down.

As the property owner, you will need to do your best to hold down the operating costs associated with the property. This does not mean skimping on necessary repairs and upkeep. On the contrary, you want to take care of problems as early as possible. Paying a heating expert to clean and maintain the furnace or boiler each year can mean big savings by extending the life of the heating system and not having to replace it for several years. Calling a roofing professional to seal leaky cracks not only prevents damp interior walls, wood, carpeting, and mold, but also allows the roofer to keep an eye on the roof and to advise you of potential future problems or when all or a portion of the roof will have to be replaced. On the other hand, it is not necessary to repaint the units every year or to remodel the kitchens and bathrooms if they are up to code and in fairly good shape.

For a specific example on how to calculate cash flow, assume that you want a minimum of $25,000 per year to supplement your self-employment earnings. This works out to $2,083 net per month that you would need to receive from one or more investment properties. If you had a triplex that provided net rental amounts of $700, $800, and $850 per month, you would be getting $2,350 per month. That is well over the minimal amount that you wanted with a nice cushion for unforeseen events. Also, know that you will be increasing the rents every year to the extent allowed by law.

Yet, that is not the end of the calculation. Now you need to work backward from the net rental amount and estimate the cost of repairs and maintenance, insurance, government fees, real property taxes, mortgage payments, and other expenses that would be your responsibility as the owner. Although you can make some of these estimates based on information from various Web sites, you will find that this is the time to contact your team of professionals for ballpark figures on the other expenses. With these estimates in hand, you can calculate what the gross rents would have to be. That number will give you an idea of the areas in which you should look for properties that command that kind of rent. Your down payment might also have to be large enough to keep the mortgage payments down.

Your cash-flow calculation will differ if you do not need money from a property now or in the near future and instead want to see a good return on your initial investment (the down payment) and equity growth. In this case, you may want to put a little money down and finance as much of the purchase price as possible. This most likely will lead to a small cash-flow amount, which can be applied to paying down the principal on the loan. In the meantime, not only is your equity growing from the pay down, it also is rising due to inflation and appreciation.

Your Net-Worth Targets

Think about how much you want to be worth in five or ten years or when you retire. Consider how much of a legacy you want to leave your children and other loved ones — whether you want to fund your children's or grandchildren's college education or buy a business.

Setting your net-worth target is as simple as this:

I want a net worth of $_____ within ___ years.

Getting to that net worth in that time period involves careful calculation of cash flow and a determination of how many properties to buy, when to buy them, how to finance and refinance them, and when to sell them, all while keeping the tax consequences of such moves in mind.

Your Tax-Shelter Requirements

Until you speak with your tax advisor, you may not fully understand or be aware of the tax-shelter benefits and consequences that come from investing in real estate. It is a good idea to know what your cash-flow needs and net-worth targets are before you have that conversation. The tax advisor can then suggest tax strategies that will help you reach your goals.

Those strategies may include buying properties that offer significant depreciation write-offs or using the 1031 tax-deferred exchange or an installment sale contract to defer capital gains from the sale of a property.

Finally, if you want to leave a legacy to someone or to make a charitable bequest, you will need to set up your estate and investments in certain ways to make sure that your wishes are carried out with as small a tax bite from Uncle Sam as possible. For this, you will need the assistance of your tax advisor, as well as an attorney who specializes in estate planning.

Additional Goals

In addition to the monetary goals that motivate your interest in real estate investment, you may have other objectives. For instance, you may want to find a building with a nice unit for yourself and your family to live in while renters in the other units pay down your mortgage on the property. Perhaps you do not want to live there now but would like to do so after you retire. At that point, if the mortgage has been paid off, the rents would generate a respectable cash flow to supplement your retirement income.

It may be that you want to find a place with a unit for your elderly parents or for other relatives to live in for free or for a reduced rent, again, with the rents from the other units paying the mortgage and operating expenses. Perhaps you want to use the income from a property for charitable purposes or to help out a relative or friend in need.

You may even be looking ahead to a time when you have several years of experience as a landlord of residential property and want to expand into the commercial rental field. For example, you may want to try your hand at triple net leasing. That is where a commercial tenant, such as a big-box store or stand-alone chain restaurant, pays a landlord monthly rent for a building, pays for the real property taxes and insurance, and is responsible for the maintenance expenses of the building. Thus, triple net refers to the net of taxes, insurance, and maintenance.

Whatever your additional goals may be, factor them into your investment plan.

Get Started

If you are serious about becoming an investor in residential properties, you must prepare yourself for that transition. Writing down your financial goals is only part of the preparation. If your credit score is likely to prevent you from obtaining financing from a lender, this is the time to rectify that. If your cash disappears into thin air each month, keep a log of how you are spending your hard-earned money, and see which expenditures can be cut down or eliminated.

Start reading the real estate classified ads and "for rent" listings in your local newspaper, or find a local real estate agent's Web site and start browsing properties on the market. Notice patterns in sales prices and rental amounts in several different areas.

Then, promise yourself you will begin working on your investment plan within a specific amount of time — months, not years, or even better, weeks, not months.

Part II

BUYING, FINANCING, AND SELLING INVESTMENT REAL ESTATE

6

FINDING PROPERTY

After you have assembled a team of experts and written an investment plan, it is time to figure out what kinds of property to consider and where they are located.

Location is important, not only in terms of the desirability of the area in which a property is situated, but also in terms of how close an investor wants to be to the property.

Invest Near or Far?

There are real estate gurus who tout the great sums that can be made by investing out of state because of the supposed inexpensiveness of properties there and the supposed booms in a segment of the population (such as retirees) that wants to live on those properties. Given the fact that real estate prices have been dropping in many areas of the country, such claims should never be taken at face value. Instead, they must be subjected to close scrutiny and independent verification. Even if the claims turn out to be true, a novice investor should consider the expense involved in traveling out of state to find property, to close on it, and to keep an eye on the company hired to manage it. Those travel expenses could eat up profits fast.

If you are new to investing in residential property, you may find it simpler to focus on your local market. After all, if you have lived there for a time, you are familiar with the area and perhaps even with local repairmen or handymen.

Study Your Market

The real estate agent on your team is an excellent resource for learning the prices of properties in your market. A well-informed real estate agent can even tell you about trends in pricing. If you do your research correctly, you should know, for example, how much a duplex goes for in the areas that you will be considering and how much is the price per unit of a triplex or a fourplex based on the number of bedrooms and bathrooms in a unit.

You will also need to know the rental rates in your target areas. This involves finding out not only what is charged by the owners who have tenants in the properties that are for sale, but also what is being charged for vacant units that are currently on the rental market. The reason for this is that the rents being charged for tenant-occupied units are likely based on what had been charged in the past, while the rates being sought for vacant units give a better picture of the current trend in rents. Current rents may be higher or lower than what is listed for properties that are for sale because the basis on which the owners set the rents may be unreliable. For example, the owner may not have raised rents sufficiently to keep up with local rental rates, or the owner may have charged the new tenants of a vacant unit the last rate that he or she was receiving without considering the actual rents of the local, current market.

The characteristics that make an area attractive for renters are the same as for homeowners: close schools, safety from crime, little street noise, access to public transportation, and proximity to parks, playgrounds, hospitals, and fire departments. Some of these characteristics will be evident from a drive in the area being considered. Local police departments can provide crime statistics for the area, and information about the public schools can be found at **www.schoolmatters.com**, a free school-evaluation service from Standard & Poor's. For anecdotal information and impressions about a neighborhood, you can speak with people who live in the area that you are considering.

Yet, it is not enough to know the current market conditions and area characteristics. You also must understand how changes in the national and local economies can affect your bottom line. By reading local newspapers, you can keep up with plans for the redevelopment of areas and the expansion of businesses. If, for example, a big-box store will be opening nearby, this can mean new jobs and an increased pool of renters. By the same token, businesses may be dying, and storefronts may be boarded up in the area. Maybe an area hospital is closing, meaning reduced healthcare services for local residents and the need to travel farther for those services.

You will also need to find out whether there are any planned changes in infrastructure that will affect the local area and whether those changes will be positive or negative. For example, a municipality might have plans to create a traffic-free zone to make shopping downtown easier or to construct a sports arena or a performing arts center in a formerly blighted area. Information on major capital expenditures such as these is available at the municipal hall and the planning department. Nevertheless, be aware that many such projects are planned and publicized but languish or never materialize.

Many chambers of commerce can also provide information about the local economy. In addition, municipal departments or agencies responsible for attracting new businesses will have information on the current state of the local economy and projections for the future.

All this information will keep an investor aware of what is happening locally. This knowledge will position him or her to jump on opportunities that come with positive developments in the economy and to protect his or her investments when negative developments are on the horizon.

Narrow Down the Target Areas

After you have a good overview of conditions in your local market, you will need to select one or more communities in which you will conduct your search for properties suitable for purchase.

One way to narrow down your target areas is by comparing the ROI in the areas in which you are considering a purchase. Select one representative type of property, such as a duplex, and find one that is on the market in each of those areas. Then calculate the ROI for each of those duplexes, using the same down payment and mortgage figures for all.

You will likely find that some areas appeal to you aesthetically or for emotional reasons but are too expensive. Other areas may offer good returns but make you feel uncomfortable. You will have to decide on a happy medium that fits your investment plan.

After you have surveyed a market, you may get a sense about the style of a building and the amenities in its units (and mobile homes) for which tenants seem ready to pay the highest rent per square foot. You can then focus on purchasing that type of property or a property that can be converted easily and at a low cost. This is one of many roads to success in residential-property investment.

You will want to look for multiunit properties that have separately metered heat, electricity, and, if possible, water. Otherwise, you as the owner will be responsible for paying those expenses, and you will have to allocate the costs to your clients through the rents you charge. Depending on the jurisdiction, you also may be required to provide or replace stoves and refrigerators. If a unit came with a washer and dryer, you would be responsible for their replacement if they stopped working.

Bargains (Practically) for the Taking

Some of the following properties may be found through the Multiple Listing Service (MLS) or with the help of a real estate agent. Others will require direct contact with the owner or the holder of the title.

Empty Buildings

An owner of an empty building has carrying costs, including property taxes, insurance, and most likely, mortgage. Those living next to empty buildings are not happy about it.

Degraded Buildings

Buildings in disrepair are an eyesore for the block on which they sit. The neighbors dislike them because they might bring down property values.

Buildings With Owners Who Live or are Moving Out of Town

Even if these houses have not yet fallen into disrepair, their owners are or will be too far away to continue keeping an eye on them.

Properties For Sale by Owners

Some owners forego the services of a real estate agent to save the expense of a commission. They reason that they can sell their property for a little less but pocket more than if they used an agent. The owner rarely has the wherewithal to properly advertise and market his or her property, with the result that the property remains unsold for a long time. But beware, because this type of owner also may have cut corners in the maintenance of the property. These potential bargains can be found by noting "For Sale by Owner" signs on the properties or by browsing newspapers or the MLS on the Internet (some FSBOs can be placed on the MLS for a fee).

Foreclosures

A property goes into foreclosure because its owner has had financial difficulties. Not only was the mortgage not paid for months, chances are, the property was not maintained for some time and therefore requires work, some of which may be extensive. There may also be second and third mortgages on the property that would need to be paid off.

Networks

Let your friends, family, acquaintances, and professional contacts, such as doctors, dentists, and attorneys, know that you are looking for investment property. To motivate them, offer a finder's fee for referral to a property that you end up buying.

Bad Figures = No Deal

No matter how you zero in on a property or what a bargain it seems to be, resist making an offer until you subject the relevant figures to your rigorous calculations.

CASE STUDY: STEPHEN DICLEMENTE

Realtor-Associate®
Re/Max Tri County
2275 State Highway 33, Suite 308
Hamilton, NJ 08690
(609) 954-2704
www.mercerhomes.net
steve@mercerhomes.net

I help home buyers and investors buy and sell properties in portions of Mercer County, New Jersey. We have strong employment here and bargain hunters from places like New York City. I believe that is why house prices in Mercer County increased 3.7 percent in 2007 although prices dropped 14 percent in southern New Jersey.

If a client asks me, I can recommend attorneys, appraisers, or other professionals. I give clients three names so that I have no conflict-of-interest problems. Also, if a client has not yet lined up financing, I can recommend at least four mortgage people; one of them will likely have a program that is suitable for the client.

I do not mind if new investors contact me as they prepare to look for properties. I listen to what they want to do, such as buy and flip or buy and hold. This information directs me to the kind of property they want. Based on my experience with other investors, I can suggest features to look for, such as separate utilities and heaters for apartments. I also give an idea of the rent amounts to expect. There are many other considerations, such as the cost of the home and how much money investors want to spend. I factor in everything to give my clients sound advice on what will give them the best deal and the best return on their investment.

My advice for new investors in rental properties is: (1) if you have financing available, this is a great time to buy because of low prices and low interest rates, (2) get the proper financing for what you are trying to do, and (3) get a home inspection.

7

FINANCING THE PURCHASE

In theory, it would be great for an investor to have the cash to buy any property and as many properties as he or she wants. In reality, few people are in a position to buy a property with their own resources. On the other hand, buying property with no financing is unnecessarily self-limiting, because it weakens the power to leverage.

The Power of Leveraging

Leverage has been hailed as one of the best advantages that investing in real estate has over other types of investing and as one of the most significant ways of fueling ROI. This praise is heaped on leveraging for two main reasons.

First, leverage, as it relates to buying real estate, occurs when an investor with a well-thought-out plan pays a small down payment on a property and finances the rest of the purchase price. The property will then produce enough income to cover the mortgage payments and operating expenses and maybe even to return some cash to the investor. In this way, the investor uses a little of his or her own cash to accomplish a great deal.

Second, the ability of an investor to use borrowed money rather than his or her own cash increases his or her buying power. In other words, after an investor has bought one property with just a little of his or her own money, he or she can go on to buy more properties in the same way.

By deciding how much to leverage and how much to pay outright in cash, an investor controls the amount of risk to which he or she is exposed.

How Much to Finance

You have found a property you like. You have run the numbers and determined that they meet the criteria of your investment plan. Next, you need to decide how much of a down payment you should offer and how much you should finance.

Richard Seltzer, an attorney and investor in rental properties, became adept at figuring out how much of a down payment he and his partners needed to make.

"We would put down 20 percent, sometimes more because the buildings were rent-controlled and to make them work, you could not put down 5 percent. Even if you got a 95 percent loan, you would have had a negative cash flow. We would raise money, sometimes 40 percent, and borrow 60 percent because we wanted to make the numbers work. We believed that the key was to slowly but surely raise the rents and improve the physical plant of the buildings and that over time their value would go up. In the meantime, the buildings were throwing off a positive cash flow of some small amount. But there was the depreciation on your personal tax returns, and when we sold the buildings, the profits sometimes were quite handsome."

An investor in residential property must determine the type of loan that best suits his or her circumstances. Following are some types of mortgage loans.

Fixed-Rate Mortgage

The interest rate on this type of loan never changes. In the early years of the loan, most of the monthly mortgage payment goes toward interest, while a small amount of the principal is paid down. The fixed monthly mortgage payment creates predictability for the borrower and a benefit as the rents rise over the years while the loan payment remains the same.

Figuring out the maximum monthly mortgage payment that a property can support is similar to figuring out cash flow, as mentioned in Chapter 2. For purposes of this exercise, assume the following numbers:

RENTS	ANNUAL	MONTHLY
Unit 1	$ 6,000	$ 500
Unit 2	$ 8,400	$ 700
Unit 3	$ 9,600	$ 800
Total rents	$24,000	$2,000
EXPENSES	**ANNUAL**	**MONTHLY**
Property taxes	$ 3,000	$ 250
Insurance	$ 2,400	$ 200
Repairs/maintenance	$ 1,200	$ 100
Sewer fee	$ 300	$ 25
Gov't fees	$ 120	$ 10
Total expenses	$ 7,020	$ 585

$24,000 total annual rents

- 7,020 total annual expenses

$16,980 yearly net available for loan payments

÷ 12 months

$ 1,415 monthly net available for loan payments

An investor who wants a positive cash flow should be careful not to obtain a mortgage loan that would consume the entire net amount available. Nevertheless, knowing the yearly and monthly net amounts available for loan payments allows the investor to calculate how much of a down payment he or she will need to make to obtain a loan that can be paid with the income from the property that is being considered. These calculations are also part of the investor's due diligence.

The term, or duration, of fixed-rate mortgages is commonly 15 or 30 years. The longer the loan term, the lower the monthly payment will be, which has a direct effect on the ROI of an investor.

One drawback to fixed-rate mortgages is finding a conventional lender, such as a bank or mortgage company, that offers them for a multiunit property that will not be occupied by the owner.

Adjustable-Rate Mortgage (ARM)

As the name suggests, the interest rate on this type of loan will not stay the same for the life of the loan. There are many varieties of ARMs, but they all fall into one of two categories. In a "no-negative amortization" ARM, the amount of the principal does not change with the loan payments. This allows the lender to protect itself in the event that market interest rates increase. There may be a rate adjustment twice a year with a maximum increase or decrease of, for example, 1 percent every six months. At the end of the term of the loan, the lender expects a "balloon" payment of the entire principal, which the borrower must make from his or her own resources or from the refinance of the loan.

In a "negative amortization" ARM, the amount of the monthly payments that the lender agrees to accept from the borrower may not be enough to satisfy the loan in a conventional 30-year term based on the interest rate being charged. In that case, the monthly shortfall is added to the amount of the principal. The borrower can pay more than the agreed-on minimum, in which case there is no negative amortization. There are caps on how much the payments can increase, and the interest rate is adjusted at longer intervals than for a no-negative amortization ARM.

There are also mortgages known as "fixed-to-ARMs" that have a fixed interest rate for one, three, five, or seven years, after which they become ARMs for the balance of the loan term. Before the cracks in some sectors of the mortgage lending industry began to show in 2006, it was relatively easy for buyers of real estate to obtain financing from conventional lenders. The buyer could make an extremely low down payment — commonly 5 percent, sometimes no down payment — and finance the balance of the purchase price with a fixed-to-ARM loan. Many first-time homeowners and investors could not resist the lure of miniscule cash outlays coupled with low monthly payments. This meant that bigger homes and investment properties were affordable.

As has been reported in the media, a convergence of circumstances disrupted those idyllic days. As the initial five-year terms of the ARMs ended, the rates were shooting up, sometimes doubling the monthly payments. At the same time, a glut developed in existing-home and new-home markets, driving prices down. For a borrower facing a balloon payment of principal, refinancing became impossible because the maximum amount that can be borrowed is by and large 80 percent of the appraised value of a property. Little, if any, of the principal was paid down under the ARM, which has left many borrowers with a mortgage debt that exceeded the value of the property.

The lesson is that investors must always keep an eye on their bottom line. Investors must use common sense and not engage in risky maneuvers that will get them in over their head. If an investment plan is sound, an investor only needs to follow it to be safe because he or she will buy only properties that generate sufficient income to pay the mortgage and the other expenses.

Borrowing Money Costs Money

Anyone who has ever bought real estate with borrowed money knows that it costs money to obtain money. There are various fees and expenses involved, and these vary widely from lender to lender. Who makes the loan and the type of loan involved affects the cost of borrowing. Conventional lenders, such as banks and mortgage companies, may charge for some items, while private parties or governmental agencies may charge for other items.

These are just some of the items for which lenders can charge:

- Loan fee/points

- Appraisal

- Credit report

- Loan processing

- Document preparation and review

- Prepaid interest

- Loan escrow

- Setup

- Warehousing

- Flood certification

- Mortgage insurance

- Tax service

- Wire transfer fee

- Overnight delivery fee

The loan fee, or "points," is the largest expense of borrowing money. One point represents 1 percent of the amount borrowed. Thus, if the amount borrowed is $100,000 and the lender charges three points:

$$\$100,000 \times 3\% = \$3,000 \text{ loan fee}$$

No-point/no-fee loans may seem attractive, if an investor can find them anymore from a conventional lender. Yet, nothing is ever truly free, and a lender is in the business of making money. Therefore, the lender will extract its fee through the closing costs or, more likely, through a higher interest rate than is charged for loans with points and regular fees. This can be an expensive proposition, because a loan fee is a one-time payment, while a higher interest rate is paid over the life of the loan. To determine whether a no-point loan makes sense, an investor must carefully evaluate whether the higher interest rate or closing costs of such a loan fit into his or her plan and needs.

Another expense associated with borrowing is private mortgage insurance (PMI). Anytime a borrower pays less than a 20 percent down payment, the lender will require him or her to pay for PMI, which is a guarantee that the lender will not lose any money on the loan if there is a foreclosure. PMI can equal one-quarter to one-half percent of the loan, and it stays in effect until 20 percent of the loan has been repaid.

Lenders require that the property that will serve as collateral for loans be surveyed. Lenders often refuse to accept surveys that were conducted for the prior owner, particularly when the surveys were done several years earlier. This means another expense for the borrower.

Conventional Lenders as Sources

Banks and mortgage lending companies are the sources of conventional loans. The borrower qualifies for such a loan if he or she is credit-worthy, which signifies to the lender that the borrower has the ability to repay the loan. The property itself qualifies if the appraiser for the lender concludes that the current market value of the property is not less than the price that was negotiated.

As noted earlier, properties with one to four units are considered residential for lending purposes, and ones with five or more units are considered commercial. Not all lenders provide financing for both categories of properties.

There are many different types of loans for the purchase of residential properties. The standard loan requires the borrower to make a 20 percent down payment on the property and to finance the remaining 80 percent with a mortgage loan. Some lenders allow the seller to finance all or a portion of the down payment or closing costs. Other lenders prohibit or insist on the right to approve secondary financing.

The mortgage landscape has changed significantly and rapidly from the heady pre-2006 days of easy credit terms. These days, an investor needs to be aware that lenders have clamped down hard on their lending practices, with the result that even individuals with the means to repay their loans are sometimes having problems obtaining mortgages due to more stringent qualifications.

Nevertheless, lenders are in the business of making money, and they may offer special mortgage programs, some for a limited time. For example, a bank may offer a special rate for mortgage loans to law enforcement officers and firefighters. Other mortgage lenders are now offering 40-year mortgages with a 4 percent down-payment requirement. Check with lenders in your area to find out about various mortgage programs for which you may qualify. Your real estate agent also is a good source for information on conventional financing.

Finally, some real estate investment experts recommend never offering to pay more of a down payment than is required by the lender or the seller. The reasoning is that the leverage created will lead to a higher percentage of ROI. Ultimately, the investor must decide on a course of action that accords with his or her investment plan.

The Government as a Source

The Federal Housing Administration (FHA), which is part of the U.S. Department of Housing and Urban Development, is a good source for financing the purchase of one- to four-unit residential properties, as long as the borrower fulfills the strict requirement of making one of the units his or her primary residence. The FHA itself does not issue mortgages; instead, it insures residential mortgage loans made by conventional lenders.

The goal of FHA loans is to make homeownership possible for people who would not qualify for a mortgage under conventional lending standards. To that end, FHA loans require only a 3 percent down payment, which means that 97 percent of the purchase price is leveraged. The interest rates and terms for FHA loans tend to be more favorable than those of conventional mortgage loans. There are limits on how much can be borrowed per number of units; investors should ask their lender about the limits that apply to their areas.

As of 2008, the FHA can insure loan amounts up to $417,000, or 100 percent of the Federal Home Loan Mortgage Corporation conforming-loan limit in high-priced areas, and up to $271,050 in lower-priced areas.

The FHA also has two financing programs for mobile homes and factory-built (prefab) housing. One loan program is for people who own the land on which the mobile home or prefab will be located, and another loan program is for the purchase of mobile homes that are or will be located in mobile-home parks. See **www.hud.gov/buying/loans.cfm**.

If you are a first-time home buyer interested in a multiunit building but lack the funds for a down payment, you are not necessarily out of luck. Several states and local governments have programs to assist with down payments and closing costs for individuals of limited resources who meet certain criteria. HUD makes it easy to find out whether a particular state offers such homeownership assistance programs by providing links to each of the states at **www.hud.gov/buying/localbuying.cfm**. Through those links, you can also find out whether a state has assistance programs for the purchase of rural property and mobile homes.

The HUD and FHA Web sites have a wealth of additional information on finding, negotiating for, and financing residential property. See **www.hud. gov** or **www.fha.gov**.

Assumable Loans as a Source

Sometimes, a seller has a mortgage loan that allows the buyer to take over the payments. This can be advantageous, particularly if the loan has been in place for several years, because the older the loan, the greater the percentage of the monthly payments that goes to paying down the principal; this makes the equity build up faster. Moreover, the buyer does not have to find financing and incur all the expenses connected with obtaining it.

With an assumable loan, there are likely some small fees involved. The buyer also must meet the same qualifications that the original borrower had to meet. Conversely, there may still be some loans, such as old FHA loans, that allow the buyer to begin making payments "subject to" the original borrower remaining responsible in case of default. Technically, these are not assumable loans because the buyer has not agreed to be responsible for the loan, and he or she could return the property to the original borrower and walk away from the debt. Of course, the buyer also would lose the down payment, any other funds that he or she may have put into the property, and all equity.

Private Financing as a Source

There may be situations in which you do not have all the money you need to buy a property, even if you qualify for a loan from a conventional lender. It is safe to say that there are no conventional lenders ready these days to provide 100 percent financing. Perhaps you cannot get a conventional mortgage loan because your credit score is not high enough to satisfy the bank, you do not want to incur all the fees and expenses of a conventional loan, you do not qualify for an FHA loan (because you do not want to live on the property you are buying, for instance), or you just need flexibility in the way the loan is structured.

Fortunately, conventional lenders and government agencies are not the only avenues to finding the money to buy a property. Financing from sources other than conventional lenders is known as creative financing. Sellers, private lenders, and other investors can finance all or part of the purchase price and even the down payment. You may have to put together financing from several sources. Just do not take on more debt than the property can support.

As you read through the following descriptions, take note that the reason this type of financing is called creative is because of the many variations that are possible.

Sellers

Some sellers are willing to accept a cash down payment and to take the rest of the purchase price in the form of a note with an attractive interest rate. The down payment, the duration of the loan, and the interest rate are the key negotiation points for the buyer. If the seller prefers more cash in hand now, offer a larger down payment. If the seller wants the loan paid off sooner, shorten the term of the note. If the seller wants a better return, offer a higher interest rate.

Whenever a seller agrees to provide you with full or partial financing, be sure to negotiate for the inclusion of a right of first refusal clause in the contract of sale. This clause grants you the right to buy the mortgage before anyone else in the event that the seller decides to sell it. An example of language that the contract should include is "Buyer shall have the right of first refusal to purchase the mortgage."

The right of first refusal can be extremely beneficial to a buyer. Let us assume that Ian Investor agrees to buy a fourplex from Sydney Seller for $300,000, and Sydney agrees to give Ian a second mortgage for $30,000 amortized over three years. Two years pass and Ian has been paying Sydney on time; the balance remaining on the second mortgage is $10,000. Sydney decides that she wants to take a luxurious Mediterranean cruise and does not want to wait another year to receive the funds she needs for the trip. She finds someone willing to pay her $6,500 for the second mortgage. Ian exercises his right of first refusal under his contract with Sydney and buys the mortgage for $6,500, saving $3,500 in principal plus interest.

The seller should not object to including a right of first refusal clause in the contract because he or she will be paid either by you or someone else. Do not hesitate to turn to an expert, such as an attorney, for the proper wording of a right of first refusal clause.

Private Lenders

There are people with money in self-directed IRAs or other accounts who may be willing to give you a short-term loan for an interest rate that is higher than what they are currently earning. Depending on how soon they need to have their money returned, you may be able to structure the loan so that you do not have to repay it until you sell the property, or you can make interest-only payments and repay the principal after a set period or when you sell the property. This type of lender frequently wants to be repaid within a shorter period of time.

Private lenders tend to be more concerned about the return *of* their money than about the return *on* their money. If you sense that a private lender is skittish and needs additional reassurance, you can secure the loan with an additional property, if you have one. Nevertheless, do not agree to an unreasonable interest rate.

There are other types of private lenders. Some provide funding for the acquisition, improvement, and refinancing of real estate as though they were conventional lenders. The financing they provide is known as hard money. These types of lenders impose higher up-front fees and interest rates than do conventional lenders; there may also be high late fees and penalties. Some of these lenders have no qualms about lending to people who cannot repay the loans, because the lenders can then foreclose on the properties.

There are people who advertise in newspapers that they have money to lend. They should be approached with caution, and an investor's attorney should carefully review all documents in connection with such a loan.

Other Investors

The seller might agree to carry a note for only part of the purchase price, and no conventional or private financing is possible, or the seller may insist on being paid in full. In either case, the buyer can consider turning to other investors to supply the needed funds. They could be relatives or friends who would welcome the opportunity to share in the profits of investing in real estate without the responsibility of finding and managing the property. Alternatively, one effective way to find investors is to advertise in newspapers. Just make sure that the investors have the money and do not have to borrow it.

Other investors who agree to provide funds for the purchase of the property would be coming in as your partners in the venture. You will need a skillfully drafted agreement and the proper form of ownership (Refer to Chapter 3). You should be prepared to show them a well-thought-out investment plan that sets out the actual figures and projections for the subject property. Demonstrate that you have anticipated how to handle situations such as repair costs that exceed projections, vacancies, and softening rental and sales markets.

You must choose your investing partners wisely. In addition to having the resources needed, a partner also should be someone with whom you can get along. In times of trouble, you will want someone who will work with you to resolve problems. You also want *silent* investors, not someone coming in telling you how to run the venture that you thought up and initiated.

Buying With No Money Down

There has been a proliferation of seminars, books, and recordings over the last couple of decades on how to buy real estate with no money down. The hook used by all these is the implication that it is easy to do and that immense profits will be generated by the investor without putting any of his or her own funds into the purchase of a property.

Although that may work some of the time, few investors understand the risks and realities involved in no-money-down deals, and not everyone has the fortitude and nerve to get into such a situation. Moreover, times have changed, and conventional mortgage lenders these days have no more tolerance for the type of risk involved in such financing schemes. With the unavailability of conventional financing, an investor will have to engage in creative financing if he or she is determined to buy with no money down.

One common mistake made by inexperienced investors is to buy properties at or near the asking price for no money down. This frequently means that the price paid is too high, which flies in the face of the cardinal truism of investing in property: you make your profit at the start by paying as little as possible for a property.

Although self-evident, it cannot be stressed enough that when you put nothing down on a property, you will owe the entire purchase price. This lack of leverage makes the terms of your loan crucial. If you fail to keep up with the payments, you will lose the property before you can make a profit from it. The property cannot sit empty for long and instead must generate enough income to allow you to repay the loan. The rent will need to be at or near market level, and you will need to have or quickly find good tenants who can pay the rent in full and on time.

Even in the changed financing landscape, it is still possible to buy a property with no money down. That is because, due to the tough economic times or a property owner's personal financial struggles, there are many types of distressed properties that are overlooked by most buyers but that present opportunities to a savvy, gutsy investor. This topic is covered in greater detail in Chapter 9.

You should be aware that the rents at distressed properties are often well below market. If you pay a discounted price for a problem property with no money down and you correct the problems — by repairing, painting, and cleaning up the property and/or evicting nonpaying or destructive tenants — you can turn a seemingly nightmare property into an attractive investment with positive cash flow and substantially increased value.

When Cash is King

When an investor has sufficient cash to make a purchase, it may be more beneficial to use that availability of cash to negotiate a better price on a property than it would be to obtain financing.

Alternatively, if there is enough time, the investor can obtain financing and have it in place by the time of the closing without jeopardizing the purchase. The seller would have no grounds to object to the source of the funding because he or she would be paid what was due, and the investor did not have a mortgage contingency clause in the contract.

If the investor plans to sell the property shortly after purchasing (called a "flip"), it might make more financial sense to pay cash for the property and not incur the fees and expenses involved with borrowing.

Even if an investor paid cash for a property and did not flip it, he or she can obtain a mortgage loan on the property later; this is a way to pull out cash from the property. The seller could take that cash and use it to buy one or more properties. Of course, the advisability of such a move is determined with reference to the investment plan.

CASE STUDY: KIM M. MCGREGOR

Granite Properties of Texas
808 W. 10th St.
Austin, TX 78701
(512) 469-0925
www.graniteproperties.com
kimm@graniteproperties.com

My day job is managing office buildings and shopping centers for a real estate company, and I invest in rental properties on my own time. It was late in my investment career that I started buying duplexes. I wish I had started investing in them soonerbecause I like their numbers better than those for single-family homes; in simplified terms, you get twice the income for about one and one-half the price.

After my wife and I bought a place on a lake about an hour from Austin, I invested in a duplex there. I later bought three brand-new duplexes from the same developer. A few years later, I sold a house in a 1031 exchange and used the proceeds as part of the down payment on six more duplexes in the same development at the lake. I think the 1031 exchange is the small-investor's friend. I rarely sell, but when I have, it has been in a 1031 exchange.

I commonly make a down payment of 25 percent to 30 percent. I prefer fixed-rate loans for either 15 or 30 years. With a strong coverage ratio like that, I can stand downtimes, vacancies, and turn-around costs. I am conservative and do not like to gamble.

The way I do the numbers, when one side of a duplex is vacant, the other side can carry the expenses for quite a while. I buy garden-style duplexes, which are prominent in this part of the Southwest. They are one-story buildings with few plumbing issues that affect both sides. There are also no common utilities, so I have no utility bills when the units are occupied.

My advice for new investors in duplexes is: (1) get all the expertise you can from others who invest in them, (2) do credit checks — even with the confidentiality issues — because they are worth the effort and pay off in the end, and (3) use a battle-tested standard lease.

8

DO YOUR DUE DILIGENCE

This chapter will reveal what due diligence is in terms of investing in residential properties. Even if time and money are scarce commodities to an investor who is just starting out, it is imperative to spend a sufficient amount of both on due diligence.

As briefly described in Chapter 2, due diligence is the thorough research, verification, and analysis of the relevant data, projections, and representations about a property. When the property is real estate, due diligence also includes having the property physically inspected by a professional and searching the public records to ascertain the state of title to the property.

Rather than a nuisance or a chore, due diligence is a series of proactive steps that investors take to protect themselves from ugly surprises. After all, you are an investor, not a gambler. You want to reduce the risk of failure, and the best way to do this is by investigating the attributes, past performance, and future potential of a property as thoroughly as possible.

Following are the steps involved in performing due diligence for most residential properties. Depending on the property and/or type of financing involved, an investor may need to take additional or different steps.

Precontract Due Diligence

An investor in residential property who is serious about succeeding has work to do, even before signing a contract to buy a property.

Investment Plan

The serious investor has prepared a real estate investment plan (or mobile home/mobile-home park investment plan) long before contacting a real estate agent to begin the search for a suitable property. The plan clearly sets forth the investor's objectives, the investment strategies for arriving at those objectives, and the strategies for when and how to exit from the investments.

Demographic Research

Being familiar with the demographics involves more than just knowing where a particular property sits. It involves knowing the types of people, homes, businesses, and social and community facilities that are present in a target neighborhood. Among other things, an investor can assess a neighborhood by:

- Population

- Trends in population growth

- Age ranges

- Income ranges

- Occupations

- Median home price

- Housing-stock age

- Trends in home values

- Apartment vacancy rates

- Rent ranges

Much of this data can be found on the Internet at sites such as **www. citydata.com** and **www.bestplaces.net**. The investor also should read the local newspapers to become familiar with the machinations of local politics, the plans of the local government, and the possible impact that these could have on a neighborhood. In addition to looking at the classified listings in newspapers, the investor needs to ask around to get an idea of the prices that properties are selling for and how much the current rents are. It also helps to drive around the neighborhood and see how the residents take care of their homes. Now is also the time to speak with an insurance agent to get an idea of the insurance premiums for rental properties in the area.

The purpose of all this information is to give the investor a panoramic view of the interconnected parts that make up a neighborhood, rather than just a snapshot of an isolated block or house in the neighborhood.

When all the pertinent information has been gathered and studied, the investor can confidently pin down the area in which to search for a property. The investor knows how much ROI he or she requires and how much to realistically expect of a property in the target area.

At that point, the investor is ready to look at properties.

Information Verification

To choose an appropriate property, an investor must have information about the location, income, features, and physical condition of a property.

After finding a property that seems to fit the criteria of location, income, size, and type, the investor must verify pertinent information before submitting an offer to buy the property. For his or her own protection, the investor must do this even when buying a rental property from a partner's relative. A serious investor is transacting a business deal, so he or she cannot afford to accept the seller's representations about what the rents are or how many units in a building are rented. Some sellers want to make their properties appear more profitable than they are. Others have only vague notions about the performance of their properties. This is why the investor must ask to see the rent rolls.

In addition, when the investor visits the property for the first time, it is a good idea to speak with the tenants if they are present. The investor should ask what the neighborhood is like, how long they have been living in their units, and whether they have had any problems in the building. The answers to these types of questions may reveal whether the tenants are withholding rent in an effort to get long-requested repairs and whether the tenants plan to leave when their lease terms are up. Real estate agents may try to discourage a buyer from asking tenants questions, but that should not stop the buyer from doing so.

This is also the time to check how the utilities are metered and to verify whether the tenants pay for their own heat, water, and utilities. The investor or the real estate agent can confirm the amount of the real estate taxes for the current year.

Postcontract Due Diligence

You have verified the rents and leases on a property that interests you. You know what the real property taxes are and how much the insurance is likely to cost. A clause in the contract specifies which appliances and other personal property are included in the sale. The seller has accepted your offer, and you have each signed a contract that has been approved by your respective attorneys.

Now, several steps must be taken almost simultaneously. Some you will take; others your attorney and your lender will take for you.

Property Inspection

As noted in Chapter 4, the buyer should hire a licensed professional property inspector to look at the property from roof to basement. If the inspector finds serious structural defects, such as a cracked foundation or a roof on the verge of collapse, this could be a deal breaker if the seller does not want to pay for repairs and the buyer is unwilling to take the property as is. A buyer should remember that it is better to walk away from a deal that is not right than to be stuck with a property that will fail to perform as required by his or her investment plan.

Note: Although a property inspection report may refer to damage from termites, conventional lenders invariably require termite inspection reports from licensed pest-control companies.

The property inspection report will include so many things that are wrong with a property that the buyer may begin to have second thoughts about going through with the purchase. There is no need to be disheartened. The inspector is just doing what he or she was hired to do — a thorough inspection — and not all the detected defects will be serious enough to warrant cancellation of the contract. For example, the inspector may find that the furnace should have a larger expansion tank than it has, even though the inspector also reports that the furnace is working just fine. This would be something to keep an eye on in the future and to discuss with the professional that the buyer will hire to perform service on the heater. The inspector should be able to provide the buyer with a ballpark estimate of the cost of repairs, but the buyer may want to follow up by contacting a handyman or contractor for a more accurate figure.

The buyer will provide his or her attorney with a copy of the inspection report and will point out problems that should be brought to the attention of the attorney for the seller. Then it is a process of negotiating what, if anything, the seller is willing to do to rectify the problems, as well as any concessions the buyer may be willing to make to allow the purchase to go through. Because this is a process of give and take, a smart buyer should allow sufficient wiggle room by including serious defects and lesser problems on the list of repairs demanded from the seller. Nevertheless, a buyer should not hesitate to ask for as many concessions as possible. In a difficult selling market, the seller may agree to an astonishing amount of repairs to save the deal if he or she is worried that the buyer will slip away.

The property inspector may notice conditions on the property that raise concerns about environmental contamination from a source that is not on the property. Alternatively, the inspector may find evidence of an abandoned oil tank buried in the yard. If so, further inspections by appropriate professionals will be required to determine the extent of contamination; for example, a buried oil tank that was never emptied may have holes from which oil seeps down to the water table. The cost of these tests will far exceed the cost of the property inspection, and it would be advisable to try to get the seller to defray some of the expense. Correcting the problems could be costly and time consuming and would fall squarely on the seller's shoulders. In that case, the seller and the buyer would have to evaluate whether it would better to let the deal die.

No matter how quickly the seller and the buyer want to close, it is advisable to put off ordering title work and a survey until the inspection report is issued. If the report reveals serious structural problems and the investor chooses to void his or her offer and cancel the contract, the unnecessary expense of title work and a survey will have been avoided.

Appraisal and Survey

As noted in Chapter 4, if a conventional lender is financing the purchase of a property, it will require a report from an appraiser to determine whether the market value of the property is at least equal to the amount of the purchase price.

A conventional lender also will require a survey if the seller cannot or does not provide a recent one. The title company also will want to see a survey. Even if a conventional lender is not providing financing, the buyer should consider ordering a survey to find out the actual boundaries of the property being bought. It is not unusual for a surveyor to find that an adjoining property is encroaching — that is, the border of an adjoining property has been extended into the other property, whether purposely or inadvertently. An encroachment commonly occurs when shrubbery spreads over two properties that may have been a single property at one time, when a building next door has been expanded, or when a fence has been put up between two properties.

Nonetheless, surveyors do not always notice encroachments, particularly if they rely on markings or measuring nails left by a previous surveyor. The only way to truly be sure of the dimensions of a property is by obtaining from the county clerk a copy of a plat that shows the lot and then going to the property to carefully compare the boundaries on the plat with the boundaries in the survey. Often, it is only the most cautious, experienced real estate investors who take the time to do this.

Examination of Seller's Books and Records

The investor must carefully review the rent rolls of a property and the leases. The rents listed on the leases should match the rent rolls. The investor must scrutinize the leases to confirm who is responsible for the heat, utilities, water, and sewer bills, as well as whether there are unusual conditions that bind the owner or the tenants. The lease also should reveal whether a tenant receives a Section 8 housing subsidy.

The investor also must find out the amounts of the security deposits being held by the seller and where they are being held. This is crucial because many states have laws that dictate the maximum amount of a security deposit that a seller may request and require a security deposit to be held in an interest-bearing bank account for the benefit of the tenant.

The seller's income and expense statement for a property for the past year or two also will give the investor insight on the property. The seller's Schedule E from the federal tax return will list fairly accurate numbers and should show whether the seller collects all the rents claimed.

The investor is also entitled to see the following records:

- Rent-collections report

- Expense report

- Utility bills, if applicable

- Notices of pending legal actions, if applicable

- Permits for work performed or being performed on the property

- Notices of code violations at the property

- Documentation of all work performed at the property during the seller's ownership

- Warranties for work performed or appliances placed at the property

Credit Reports on Tenants

An investor should consider ordering credit reports for the tenants who already live on the property being considered. This is a way of gauging whether a tenant is likely to pay the rent on time. Nonetheless, the investor must decide the cost-effectiveness of this step, particularly if a tenant is a longtime resident at the property and the seller's records indicate no payment problems. The privacy laws have also changed and now impose strict security requirements that an investor working from home will not be able to meet.

Confirmation of Property Taxes and Other Expenses

At this stage, the real estate agent can reconfirm how much the property taxes are. The attorney who represents the investor also will contact the local tax office to confirm whether the taxes are current or in arrears.

Insurance

A conventional lender will require proof of insurance on the property and proof that the premium for an entire year has been paid. Even if the financing comes from a private source or the transaction is an all-cash deal, the investor will want to have the property covered by adequate insurance.

Title Search and Title Insurance

The buyer's attorney will order the title work on a property. As shown in Chapter 4, the title insurance company will look for all the recorded deeds, mortgages, liens, easements, rights-of-way, and other interests in the property. Any old, open mortgages or liens against a property are considered "clouds on title" that prevent the buyer from obtaining ownership free and clear of any possible challenge by others. The title company and the buyer's attorney will insist that all open items be closed before the purchase can be completed.

After the title company is satisfied that the seller can pass clear title to the buyer, it will issue a policy of title insurance that protects the buyer from claims that the title that passed was not marketable and free of encumbrances.

Final Words on Due Diligence

The due diligence period between the signing of the contract and the closing of title is the investor's last opportunity to find out the inner workings of the property under consideration. Throughout the due diligence period, the investor must keep asking questions until satisfactory answers in writing are forthcoming. A seller who stonewalls may do an about-face when the investor displays a willingness to allow the deal to collapse.

If the review of the books and records or the inspection of the property reveals shortcomings or substantial problems, the investor should not hesitate to request credits against the purchase price or other concessions from the seller. If the parties cannot work out their differences, the investor, through his or her attorney, may cancel the contract. It may take several weeks for the seller to realize that the deal is truly dead and to authorize the return of the down payment to the investor, but the investor should rest assured that it would have been a costly mistake to proceed with that particular transaction.

On the other hand, you, as an investor, may be fortunate (and skilled) enough to end up the owner of a property that meets the criteria of your investment plan. If that is the case, congratulations. You have overcome your hesitations and are on the road to realizing your financial security.

CASE STUDY: REBECCA MCLEAN

Executive Director
National Real Estate Investors Association
525 West 5th St., Suite 1A
Covington, KY 41011
(888) 762-7342
www.NationalREIA.com

The National REIA provides networking,
support, and educational programs for local real
estate investor associations and their members. The National REIA has
existedsince 1985 but took its current name and acquired nonprofit status
in 1993. Currently, the National REIA has about 250 member groups that are
composed of approximately 40,000 individual investors.

Individuals have much to gain by belonging to local real estate investor
associations. They can learn about deals that are available, problems
that other investors are facing, and how to avoid those problems. The
biggest benefit is that investors become aware of the changing laws and
the state of the economy. In addition, most local groups offer informal,
buddy-type mentoring in which more experienced investors are available
to advise newer investors on how to handle problems that come up.

The National REIA is also in favor of professional housing provider (PHP)
certification. We believe that good businesspersons, regardless of the
industry they are in, must possess some basic information. For real estate
investors, there are basics you need to know if you are buying and holding
or buying and selling. Ethics is a cornerstone of PHP certification, as are
the laws that affect investors, which is everything from fair housing laws to
Environmental Protection Agency regulations on lead, asbestos, and mold.
Other parts of the PHP certification program include information that keeps
an investor from making bad decisions or being taken advantage of —
such as negotiations and appraisals — and hands-on rehabilitation, tenant
laws, insurance, taxes, and other topics that help an investor do business.

For new investors in real estate my advice is (1) find people who have
invested and talk with them to keep from making mistakes before you are
too far into your investment career, and (2) do your due diligence to avoid
unpleasant fallout.

9

ARE FIXER-UPPERS FOR YOU?

This chapter reveals the advantages and pitfalls of investing in properties that are either in need of upgrades or owned by individuals who are unable or unwilling to continue holding on to the properties. For purposes of simplicity, these two types of property are referred to as fixer-uppers — houses that are run down in appearance, poorly maintained, or otherwise distressed.

Various real estate investors have written books in which they describe the fixer-upper as one of the best and surest ways to create wealth. The basic premise is that

- Owners of properties with problems are "highly motivated" to get rid of them

- A savvy investor should be able to look at a distressed property and calculate how much he or she could command in rent or purchase price if the property were repaired, upgraded, and prettied up

- The investor should be able to negotiate a deeply discounted price for the property, based on its current condition

The real question is whether fixer-uppers are for *you*. You must decide whether you have the interest, time, and fortitude to undertake the repair, renovation, or upgrade of a rental property. You must also assess whether the renovation can be done through your own efforts and skills or through those of contractors or handymen whom you hire.

Before you decide how to answer, consider the different ways in which a property is distressed and what is involved in bringing a property out of distress and making it more valuable and attractive to others who will rent or buy it from you.

Types of Fixer-Upper Properties

Individuals who want to include fixer-uppers in their investment plans must steel themselves as they look at one problem-plagued property after another. They must always remember that the true value of such a property lies beneath its troubled surface.

These are some examples of properties that qualify for fixer-upper status:

- Houses with outmoded designs or features

- Badly neglected houses with careless tenants

- Properties made unattractive by old, rusty cars, appliances, and other junk that belongs to tenants and others

- Property that has been vacant for a long time

- Properties repossessed by banks, in foreclosure, or the subjects of bankruptcy proceedings

- New houses that are incomplete because the contractor or owner is in financial distress or has lost interest in the project because of a changed real estate climate

Properties sometimes slip into distressed status due to outside forces and the passage of time, but ultimately, it is because of the type of owner involved.

The owner may live far away or may have relocated to another state because of work and may be carrying two mortgages. Perhaps the owner is too advanced in age or too disabled to properly care for the property. The owner may be preoccupied by a divorce, illness in the family, or severe financial crisis. The owner may be retired and on a limited income or may have died and left the property to heirs who prefer to have the cash. Or it could be that the owner has lost his or her job and needs to liquidate nonperforming assets.

The investor should be looking for a discount of 20 to 50 percent under the potential market value, depending on what is wrong with the property or the type of distress the owner is in. This may require some tough negotiations with an owner who does not grasp why his or her run-down property cannot command a price in the range of prices enjoyed by better-kept properties in the neighborhood.

Obviously, investing in properties that have a slew of physical (and often tenant) problems is not for the faint of heart. It takes drive, determination, ability, and funds to correct problems at distressed properties. Most investors prefer to just collect the rent checks each month. Largely for these reasons, investors will find much less competition for run-down residential properties than they will for properties that are in good shape.

Outmoded Design

When the times leave a house behind, so does the retail market. The design and style of a house may become outmoded because of the changing tastes and needs of prospective buyers. Likewise, the outdated systems and appliances in a house also contribute to the loss in value of a property. With the availability of so many other properties that have kept up with the times, the average buyer will not consider an older, seemingly obsolete property. For the savvy investor, however, these types of properties are diamonds in the rough that can be refined to raise their inherent value.

A property can become outmoded due to the lack of a central heating system or the presence of an old electrical system that cannot support today's ranges, refrigerators, wide-screen televisions, and computers. A house with these basic deficiencies is likely to have others as well. The layout, cabinetry, and lighting of the kitchen may be poor, and the color scheme of the tub, toilet, and tile in the bathroom may reflect the taste of a past decade.

Although a property with outmoded design or features may present an opportunity to buy low and sell high after some adjustments, investors need to be aware of where the property is located. It makes no sense to update a property that is surrounded by other distressed properties, because few home buyers and renters will want to live there, no matter how nice and modern a property looks. On the other hand, if the other properties nearby are in good, clean condition and their value reflects this, an investor can feel confident that the changes made to an outmoded property will make its value rise.

Another category of outmoded design is the single-family house that can be converted into a two- or three-family house. If this is possible, it will be a surefire way to add value to the property. For example, a two-story, three-bedroom, single-family house in Trenton, New Jersey, may rent for $1,100 per month, depending on the neighborhood. That same house, divided into two residential units with two bedrooms, may command $725 to $900 per month for each apartment. An investor must weigh the conversion option carefully, keeping in mind not only the costs of doing so, but the time and effort that will be required to convince the local zoning and planning boards to allow the conversion. The case for conversion will be strengthened if the investor can show that at sometime in the past the house or others near it had been subdivided into more than one unit.

Cosmetic Damage

There is a wide spectrum of problems that can plague a property.

At one end of the spectrum is cosmetic damage, which is merely superficial damage to a property. Correcting the damage may involve changing carpet or linoleum, washing and painting grimy walls, thoroughly cleaning and disinfecting a neglected kitchen or bathroom, or mowing the back yard and cutting down overgrown vegetation. Depending on what kind of neighborhood it is in, a house with these types of cosmetic defects can present an investor with a guaranteed opportunity for profit; because the materials needed should not be expensive, the investor may be able to do some, if not all, of the work, and it should be inexpensive to hire people to do the jobs that the investor cannot or will not do.

Yet, the easier the problems at a property are to solve, the smaller the profit margin is likely to be. In other words, the ROI on a house that simply needs a fresh coat of paint on the walls is likely to be significantly less than on a house that needs new flooring or a new roof.

Related to cosmetic damage is tenant messiness. A property in an acceptable area may be commanding below-market rents because the tenants have been allowed to be sloppy. If an investor buys such a property, the first step will be to clean up the property, tow away the junk cars and other debris that give a bad first impression, and raise the rents to a marketable rate, to the extent permitted by local laws. All leases that come up for renewal must specify what activities on or toward the property will and will not be tolerated. Nonpaying tenants will have to be evicted, and others will move out on their own when they see a change in regime that does not tolerate their messy ways. An investor who gets rid of undesirable tenants will quickly see the value of the property rise. A better class of tenant will be attracted to the property, and the higher rents that can be requested will mean an increase in the cash flow.

Serious Faults

On the other side of the spectrum are properties with defects that may not be worth the expenditure of time and money needed to correct them. Some of those defects are:

- Buckling or cracked basement walls (signaling problems with the foundation)

- Extensive fire and/or water damage

- Extensive mold infestation

- Asbestos in the floor or ceiling tiles or other large areas

- Outdated electrical wiring or plumbing throughout the house

Whether it makes sense to pursue the purchase of a property with one or more of these defects will depend on the rigorous calculations and available resources of the investor. These resources include funds from the investor's own pocket, from government grants for property rehabilitation, or from secondary financing. But they might also include the access that the investor has to capable, trustworthy professionals who can correct the defects for a little more than the cost of materials. For example, the investor may have a relative who is a licensed electrician or a cousin who is certified in asbestos removal. An even better situation would be if it is the investor who has the necessary skills to handle the defects effectively.

Foreclosed Properties

Let us examine the four phases of the foreclosure process and how investors go about locating properties in each of those phases.

(1) **The preforeclosure phase**. A homeowner is falling more behind in making the monthly mortgage payments, and the lender begins to realize that it will have to initiate a foreclosure action. Nothing would please the lender more than for the monthly payments to be brought up to date. Instead, the homeowner is also likely to be falling behind on other debts, such as credit-card and utility bills. An investor can find out whether a property is in the preforeclosure phase by checking the public records. Some states require creditors of homeowners/debtors to file a notice of default in the county where a property is located; other states require the filing of a *lis pendens*. These documents serve as formal notice to the public that the debtor is in default and that the creditor intends to bring legal action against the debtor. Instead of personally searching the public records for these types of notices, an investor can either read the public notices filed in the local newspapers or subscribe to a service that can furnish the information.

(2) **The sheriff's sale phase**. By this point, a court has entered a judgment of foreclosure in favor of the mortgage lender, and the sheriff is auctioning the property at a public sale, where the highest bidder is often the lender. Almost all the rights of the homeowner are terminated by the sale. The lender that initiated the foreclosure proceedings receives the proceeds from the sale; this lender is also the one that has the first mortgage on the property. If the proceeds are enough to pay off the first mortgage, any remaining proceeds go to settling the other obligations in the order in which they were recorded, and then to the homeowner. Some states allow a lender who is not fully satisfied to sue the debtor for a deficiency judgment to recover the difference between the total amount owed and the amount collected at the auction. Investors can find out about sheriff's sales by looking for

notices of sale at the county courthouse where the sales will take place. The notices are also published in local newspapers. Alternatively, subscription services available in some areas can provide electronic notices of sheriff's sales.

(3) **The redemption phase**. This is the period during which a homeowner in some states has the final opportunity to get back the property, despite the foreclosure judgment, the sheriff's sale, and the passing of ownership to the highest bidder. The homeowner has a specific time period (up to one year in some states) to exercise the right of redemption, which is the right to get back the property in exchange for paying all the money owed on the mortgage loan, the costs of the court proceedings and the sheriff's sale, and other fees. Although homeowners often lack the resources to exercise their right of redemption, the successful bidder who owns the property may not sell it until the redemption period ends. In the meantime, the homeowner may be living on the property without paying for it. Investors need to know that in a number of states, the homeowner may sell or assign the right of redemption in much the same way that an option can be sold to purchase property for a predetermined price. For a few thousand dollars, an investor can get a homeowner to agree to move off the property and sell the right to redeem it. To find out about properties in the redemption phase, an investor can check the public records at the courthouse where the sheriff's sale took place, check newspapers for legal notices, or use subscription services that specialize in this type of data.

(4) **The postforeclosure phase**. By now, the redemption phase has ended and the homeowner has lost all rights and claims to the property. If the successful bidder at the sheriff's sale was the lender that initiated the foreclosure, the lender now owns the property. The lender will list the property in its books as real estate owned (REO), which is a nonperforming asset for the lender. Few lenders publicize their REOs, but they may have a person, or even a department, to handle the REO

portfolio. Lenders use a network of private investors or of real estate agents to dispose of their REOs. This means that an investor can find properties to purchase by establishing relationships with several lenders to become part of the network of investors and by finding real estate agents who specialize in REOs. There are also online services that can alert investors about the availability of REOs, although the information is not always up to date.

Distressed Developers and Builders

When a real estate developer decides that the best and highest-value use of a particular parcel of land is for residential housing (or some other type of construction), the developer has assessed what the demands of the market are for that area. That assessment may hold true as the developer spends thousands of dollars in fees for architects, engineers, lawyers, and other professionals, as well as for applications to government bodies for site plan approval, zoning variances, and construction permits. With all the money, time, and effort that is expended even before the ground is broken at the site, the developer needs to maintain a belief in the accuracy of its assessment of market demand as the construction phase of a project gets under way. Faint signs of a changing market climate tend to be ignored or explained away.

Developers like to presell lots to raise cash to pay down the debts incurred in the preconstruction phase. Often, the builder will buy many, or even all, of the lots. Unfortunately, it is common that the early warning signs of economic troubles develop quickly into a full-blown reality for developers and builders by the time a project is completed — or even before completion. Suddenly, the developer and builder realize that even if they finish the houses, they are likely to sit vacant for months, even years, because there will be few buyers. Lagging sales make it difficult for the developer to pay its lenders. The same is true for the builder that has borrowed funds to buy lots from the developer.

As the months pass and buyers fail to materialize, the developer and the builder fall further into financial distress. Now the goal becomes to dispose of the unwanted lots, rather than to realize a profit. Developers and builders anxious to raise funds to pay off the debts incurred in their project will be willing to make considerable concessions to investors who express an interest in taking properties off their hands.

Builders also may become distressed and have to cease construction when the cost of one or more of the raw building materials rises and there is an insufficient inflow of cash to pay the higher prices. To make up this cash shortfall, a builder may be forced to sell several of the unfinished houses at a discount.

The investor who plans to buy unfinished houses must have financing in place, although distressed developers and builders may offer deep discounts for cash deals. The investor also must have an accurate idea of how much it will cost to complete the houses. Unless the investor is experienced in the construction trades, he or she will need the help of an expert, such as a builder, to learn what will be involved and how much it will cost to complete the construction. Alternatively, the investor should have a plan for quickly reselling the houses in their unfinished state.

If a developer or builder manages to complete the construction of the planned houses and the market for them has deteriorated, the result will be a backlog of inventory. At the same time, the interest, taxes, insurance, utilities, and other carrying costs will mount. The time will come when the developer or builder calculates that it is more prudent to sell the houses in its inventory at a discount than to keep them and their carrying costs. For the investor, this means getting a brand-new house at a favorable price that will be worth much more in a real estate market upturn.

As attractive as these purchases may be, they are unlikely to involve multifamily homes, except possibly in vacation areas, such as near lakes.

The vast majority of new construction involves single-family homes. Nonetheless, an investor may be able to buy new houses at a deep discount, sell them for a tidy profit, and use the proceeds to buy other properties, including multifamily homes. The point is that when an investor starts working his or her plan for investing in multifamily housing, other related opportunities to hasten the achievement of the financial goals in the plan will present themselves.

Keep Your Head Above Water

You may decide to take on a property with some serious defects. Or it may be that a property that interests you does not have serious structural, asbestos, or mold problems and instead has a large number of superficial defects or a mix of superficial and serious defects.

The important thing is not to get in over your head. This is yet another way that an investor in residential properties can control the level of risk that he or she wants to undertake. There is a learning curve involved for those who want to succeed as investors in fixer-uppers. Thus, it may not be ideal for a first-time investor to take on a property that has many problems to resolve; such a challenge may be more appropriate for an investor who has had experience with two or three properties with fewer problems.

Inspect, Then Project

As with any other prospect, you must have the distressed property inspected thoroughly by a professional as part of your due diligence. Explain to the inspector that you are considering buying the property if it has only cosmetic damage. After the inspector issues the report listing the various items that are wrong with the property, confirm that those items are easy and relatively inexpensive to correct.

Then make an educated estimate of the sale price after the property has been fixed up, based on what similar houses in good condition are selling for in the immediate area. If you plan to hold on to the property for a few years, for the cash flow or other reasons, you also must be careful to research whether there are tenants who will want to live in a renovated home for the rents that you would need to charge to make a profit.

When projecting the sale of a fixer-upper, do not make the amateurish mistake of buying a house for, say, $80,000, fixing it for $20,000, then adding a figure that appeals to you, such as $30,000, to come up with an ideal sales price of $130,000. If other similar houses are selling for only $95,000, your pricing will be way off. You must investigate the sale price of other similar houses in the same area as your investment property.

Haggle, But be Prepared to Walk

You may have found a property that has several serious defects that will require extensive repairs and cash outlay. When you run the numbers, you find that the buying costs plus the fix-up costs are more than the estimated resale value of the property, if it was in the best condition supported by the market in which it is located. Although it may seem to be time to forget about the property, this is not necessarily true.

You can go back to the owner and try to renegotiate. Stress that the price is too high and the needed repairs are too numerous to allow you to make a reasonable profit on the property. If the seller still continues to refuse to accept a price that makes sense to you, then it is time to walk away. Each property is unique, but there are many on the market at any given time. Keep looking; you may find a distressed property that fits your needs.

Avoid Over-Renovating

When a property is yours and you start renovations, it is understandable that you want to spruce it up to a level that you personally would find comfortable. You must resist the temptation to overspend on fix-ups. The over-improvement of rental properties will erode your ROI. Remember, you are not the one who will be living there. Therefore, you need to make only the upgrades or renovations that will make the property more appealing to renters or purchasers and that will prevent the property from losing value.

Several experts have suggested that an owner should be able to increase the rents or enhance the value of a property by $2 for every $1 spent on improvements.

Those figures may not hold up in all areas. The important factor in determining how much to renovate is the location of the property. Location determines value. If your property is in a neighborhood of low-priced homes and rents, do not fill the house with top-of-the-line cabinetry, countertops, flooring, and appliances. The market in that location will not support that type of extravagant improvement.

The lesson for the investor is to determine the top sale price or rent that a property can command, if fixed up, and to make upgrades and repairs up to that level. Anything more will be a waste of money and effort.

Seller Financing

Fixer-uppers present problems to their owners. Because few people will even bother looking at fixer-uppers, an owner of one may consider himself or herself lucky when an investor takes the time to look at it and then expresses an interest in taking the problem away. If financially able to do so, an owner may be willing to accept the investor's offer at a discounted price. Sellers of run-down properties may go so far as to provide as much as 100 percent financing to an interested buyer.

Aside from the obvious leverage benefit of 100 percent seller financing, such a deal is good because the time and effort expended by an investor to fix a problem-plagued property is worth more than the cash value of a down payment. The ultimate payoff for the investor is a property of substantially higher value.

Even if the seller insists on having some cash, he or she may be willing to accept a small down payment and take back a note and mortgage for the balance of the purchase price, if the investor can show on paper that the interest that the seller would earn on the note exceeds what could be earned from a conservative investment vehicle, such as a savings account, a certificate of deposit, or a money market account.

Investors in distressed properties who are not paying cash may want to do all they can to convince the seller to finance at least a part of the purchase price. Particularly in the current climate of restrictive financing, it is difficult, if not impossible, to find a conventional lender that is willing to finance the purchase of run-down property. Look at it from the lender's point of view: there would be appraisal problems, finding insurance would be a challenge, and, in the event of a foreclosure, the lender would be stuck with an unattractive property in its inventory. Conventional lenders are not in the business of fixing up properties for resale.

Do it Yourself or Hire Help?

For the beginning investor in fixer-uppers, it is advisable that the first few properties acquired have only simple problems. Minor repairs, painting, and tending the lawn and yard may cost little and give an instant "face lift" to a rental property. Moreover, the investor may possess the skills needed for those improvements.

For investors doing the repair work themselves rather than having contractors do it, there will be less out-of-pocket outlay. But investors also must factor in the time involved. An investor must decide whether it makes sense to keep a property off the rental market for three, six, or more months while spending all his or her free evenings, weekends, and holidays toiling away to save the few thousand dollars that capable contractors or handymen would charge for work they could complete in a week or two. The rent lost for the period that the property is off the market is gone forever, and the investor would be only marginally closer, at best, to achieving the goals of his or her investment plan. Neither can the investor ignore the tax deductions that are available for paying others to do repairs at an investment property.

Anna Mills, who has repaired and renovated her properties in her 33-year career as an investor in residential properties, emphasized:

"If I could teach new investors anything, it would be that time is money. You cannot take three or four months to rehab a property and then another four months to get it rented out. That is the kind of thing that will kill you. Not only will you lose your enthusiasm by having the property off the market for so long, you will also be losing the income and footing the gas, electric, water, and other holding expenses."

If an investor decides to hire a contractor, the investor should ask people he or she knows, and even the real estate agent used for the purchase, for the names of licensed, competent, and reliable contractors they can recommend. It is advisable to get at least three names, because the investor will need to have at least three bids. All the bids should be for the same work; this is the only way to compare prices.

In time, as the investor watches handymen and contractors work, the investor will learn how much time a job should take, which materials are needed, and how much a job should cost. This is valuable information, because it can save the investor from dealing with shady laborers and overpricing in the future.

If the investor already knows the going rates for the particular job at hand and a contractor or handyman has given the investor a competitive bid, the investor can tell the contractor or handyman that the job will be given to him or her if the price can be lowered. Ten percent is a reasonable amount to expect to be knocked off the price. If the contractor or handyman agrees, the investor will have saved the time and trouble of tracking down additional bids. (Find more on contractors and handymen in Part III.)

No matter who does the work at the property, the investor must be sure to obtain all the permits required by the municipality in which the property is located. The investor also must make sure that all the improvements to the property comply with the applicable building and occupancy codes.

If Fixer-Uppers are Not For You

After reading the information in this chapter, you may decide that you want nothing to do with fixer-uppers. There is no need for concern. Most other people do not want them either, which is why investors find little competition for this type of property.

Your better course could be to look for properties with distressed owners. Such properties tend to be priced below their actual value, which presents attractive opportunities for investors.

Perhaps you do not want to deal with owners in distress. Instead of looking at how you could help someone in trouble, you think you would be taking advantage of other people's difficulties.

Reluctance to consider properties that need fixing up or that have owners who are anxious to sell, means that you will be looking for properties that are selling at or close to retail price because they are not undervalued. You have a duty to yourself, your partners, and your investment plan to get the best deal possible, but you will be paying more for a property that is already in good condition.

CASE STUDY: MIKE HURNEY

Director
Massachusetts Real Estate Investors
Association
www.massrealestate.net
Mike@MassRealEstate.net
(781) 405-1845 (Cell)

I started investing in real estate in 1982, but I consider myself a beginner because there is always something more to learn or something I forgot. I invest in single-family, two-family, and three-family homes, and they are within driving distance of my home. In my book, *How to Become a Real Estate Investor in 12 Tough Lessons* and in my classes on real estate investing, I advocate buying in your own town.

I buy properties to fix up and sell; my Plan B is to rent them out. I buy and sell all the time. Like in dollar-cost averaging: I may buy in a high market but I also sell in a high market, and when I sell in a low market I am also buying in a low market. It is almost impossible to time the market.

I used to buy properties that were very run down. But as you go along and develop self-confidence, you end up looking for distressed sellers, not distressed properties. Investors need to know what portion of a market is moving at a given time and concentrate on that. For example, after hearing from so many in my real estate investors group (**massrealestate.net**) that nothing was moving, I analyzed the market in one Massachusetts town. I found that starter houses, high-end houses, and condos were not selling but that move-up houses — where someone moves up from a starter home to a larger home — were doing well.

In addition to investing in properties, I run Entrust New England, LLC, which is a self-directed individual retirement account company that allows people to use their IRA funds to buy properties and options and do private placements, lending, and other real-estate related deals.

My advice to those interested in investing in properties is (1) just do it, and (2) when you find a property you like, make an offer; surprisingly, that is the most difficult hurdle for people to overcome.

10

GOVERNMENT PROGRAMS FOR PROPERTY REHABILITATION

For years, late-night infomercials on television have been urging viewers to sign up for free seminars on how to find out about government programs that provide funding to buy and fix up properties. This is what happens at these "seminars:" a well-dressed speaker tells you what you already heard in the infomercial. Several other well-dressed individuals hand you colorful booklets and maybe even a CD with extremely general information. You are herded to a table where smiling assistants are ready to sign you up, at a cost of several hundred dollars, for a course, books, and other materials that "reveal" what those government programs are.

When it comes to locating government programs for the rehabilitation of residential real estate, it is not necessary to spend a dime. There is also no secret to reveal — the federal government makes funds available for individuals who buy one- to four-family houses that need repairs. The "catch" is that the owner must live in one of the units. If the owner does not mind this requirement and otherwise qualifies for one of these property rehabilitation programs, he or she will find that the terms are reasonable and offer a terrific way to get started as an investor, not only in multiunit rental housing, but also in fixer-uppers.

HUD/FHA Rehabilitation Programs

Ordinarily, when an individual wants to buy a house that needs repairs or upgrades, a conventional lender will not issue a mortgage until the repairs or upgrades are made. The U.S. Department of Housing and Urban Development (HUD) recognizes that this puts the buyer in a bind, because no changes can be made to a property until the buyer owns it.

An individual may need to find interim financing for the purchase of a property, additional interim financing for the rehabilitation work, and after the rehabilitation is complete, a permanent mortgage to pay off the interim loans. The interim financing is frequently at high interest rates and for short terms.

HUD has developed several programs administered by the Federal Housing Authority (FHA) that allow individuals to both buy and rehabilitate a qualifying property with just one long-term mortgage loan at a competitive interest rate. Although the funds do not come from the government, the government guarantees the loans, which makes them palatable to otherwise reluctant banks and mortgage companies.

The Section 203(k) Program

The Section 203(k) program is the key program offered by HUD for the rehabilitation and repair of owner-occupied homes, the revitalization of neighborhoods and communities, and the augmentation of opportunities for homeownership. The program derives from Section 203(k) of the National Housing Act, which was designed to permit HUD "to promote and facilitate the restoration and preservation of the Nation's existing housing stock."

To that end, the Section 203(k) program allows a home buyer to obtain an FHA-backed loan from a conventional lender for the purchase of a fixer-upper (also called a "handyman special"), plus the cost of repairs and improvements. The borrower must make a down payment of only 3 percent of the total of the purchase price and repair costs.

The amount of the loan is calculated on the basis of the estimated value of the property after rehabilitation. The maximum amount of the mortgage loan is the lesser of (a) the as-is value of the property before rehabilitation, plus the cost of rehabilitation, minus the down payment or (b) 110 percent of the expected market value of the property after rehabilitation, minus the down payment.

The minimum amount of allowable repairs or improvements to an existing structure is $5,000. Although minor or cosmetic repairs do not qualify on their own, they can be added to the minimum required amount.

The property that a buyer wants to finance through the Section 203(k) program must have been completed for at least one year and must be a one- to four-family house. The number of units in the house must be in accordance with the local zoning requirements. On the other hand, if the house is to be demolished or razed as part of the rehabilitation, the property can still qualify for the Section 203(k) program if a portion of the existing foundation stays in place.

A Section 203(k) loan also can be used to convert a one-family house to a two- to four-family house or to decrease a multiunit building to a one- to four-family house.

Moreover, the Section 203(k) program is available for a mixed-use property. This can be a boon to an investor who has located an undervalued but promising property that has a storefront and up to four residential units. The conditions for eligibility of a mixed-use property are that:

- The floor area of no more than 25 percent of a one-story building,

33 percent of a three-story building, or 49 percent of a two-story building is used for "commercial (storefront) purposes"

- The commercial use does not affect the health and safety of those who live in the residential portion of the building

- The Section 203(k) funds are used exclusively for the "residential functions" of the building and the access areas of the residential portion of the building

After entering into a contract for a fixer-upper, the buyer goes to a lender approved by the FHA with a detailed proposal of the needed repairs or improvements. After the issuance of an appraisal that determines what the value of the property would be after the renovations and a determination of the buyer's credit-worthiness, the loan is made for an amount that covers the purchase price, the renovation costs, and the allowable closing costs. The loan also will include a contingency reserve of 10 to 20 percent of the total remodeling costs to cover additional work that was not included in the original proposal.

The funds that remain after the seller is paid the purchase price go into escrow for the remodeling expenses incurred during the rehabilitation period. These escrowed funds are released to the contractor through a series of draws for the completed work.

The list of repairs and improvements that are acceptable as part of the $5,000 minimum requirement is extensive. It includes:

- Structural changes and reconstruction: for example, repair/replacement of structural damage, additions to the structure, chimney repair, addition of a bathroom, finishing of attics or basements, and treatment for insect infestation

- Remodeling kitchens and bathrooms and the permanent installation of appliances, such as built-in ranges or ovens, dishwashers, or microwave ovens

- Elimination of health and safety hazards, such as lead-based paint problems on pre-1978 houses

- New exterior siding or addition of a second story, covered porch, or attached carport

- Reconditioning or replacement of plumbing, heating, electrical, and air-conditioning systems

- Roof and gutter replacement or repair

- Flooring and carpeting

- Major landscape work and site improvement, such as patios and decks

- Improvements for accessibility to disabled persons

The expenses that can be included in the rehabilitation costs include:

- Materials

- Labor

- Contingency reserve

- Overhead and construction profit

- Maximum six months of mortgage payments

- Permits

- Home inspection fees

- Architectural or engineering fees

The Section 203(k) program also takes into account the desirability of alternative energy sources and energy-conservation measures. Thus, the mortgage may be increased up to 20 percent for the installation of solar energy equipment. In addition, the FHA Energy Efficient Mortgage program allows a borrower to finance into the mortgage 100 percent of the expense of cost-effective energy efficiency improvements, subject to specific dollar limits, without an appraisal of the energy improvements and without the additional credit qualification of the borrower. These costs are limited to the greater of either 5 percent of the value of the property (up to $8,000) or $4,000.

Homeowners who bought properties with cash also can take advantage of the Section 203(k) program by refinancing their mortgage loans within six months of purchase. Cash back to the owner is allowed, minus any down-payment and closing-cost requirements for the Section 203(k) loan.

The "Streamline (k)" Program

The recent Streamline (k) Limited Repair program allows purchasers to finance up to an additional $35,000 in FHA-insured proceeds into their purchase-money mortgages for upgrades or improvements to a house before moving in. The program is meant to allow new owners to tap into cash for repairs or improvements "quickly and easily."

203(b) Program

Similar to the Section 203(k) program, the Section 203(b) program makes available FHA-guaranteed mortgage loans for the price of purchasing a property plus repairs of less than $5,000.

Other Federal Programs

Title I Property Improvement Loan Insurance

The Title I program insures loans given by private lenders for "light to moderate" rehabilitation of properties and the construction of nonresidential buildings on the property.

Administered by the FHA, the program insures property rehabilitation loans for up to 20 years on single- or multifamily properties and manufactured homes. The maximum loan amount for the rehabilitation of a multifamily property is $12,000 per unit, for a total of $60,000 for a building. The fixed-rate loan is set at market interest rates. HUD does not subsidize the interest rate, but there are local communities that participate in housing rehabilitation programs which provide property-improvement loans at reduced rates through Title I lenders. The FHA insures private lenders against the risk of default by the borrower for up to 90 percent of a single loan. The annual premium charged to the borrower for this insurance is $1 per $100 of the loan amount.

The owner of the property, the person who leases the property, or an individual who is buying the property under a land installment contract is eligible for a Title I-insured loan. The proceeds of the loan may be used for "permanent property improvements that protect or improve the basic livability or utility of the property" and for fire-safety equipment.

USDA Programs

The Rural Development program of the U.S. Department of Agriculture is responsible for the economic and community development of small towns and rural areas. The Rural Development program is administered by three distinct services, including the Rural Housing Service (RHS). RHS provides direct loans and loan guarantees for single-family homeownership and multifamily housing, including home improvement loans and grants to eligible "very low income homeowners."

The Section 538 Guaranteed Rural Rental Housing program aims to increase the number of affordable multifamily units through partnerships of RHA and major lenders, state and local housing finance agencies, and bond issuers. Qualified lenders can provide loans at fixed interest rates for multifamily projects that require new construction or that involve purchase and rehabilitation in eligible areas. The loan-to-value ratio can be 90 percent or less for loans to for-profit entities. Lenders are given guarantees of up to 90 percent against loan losses. The loan proceeds can be used for:

- New construction or moderate or substantial rehabilitation

- Acquisition of buildings that meet "special housing needs"

- Construction and permanent loan combinations

- Construction of a wide variety of housing, including mobile homes

Borrowers who are eligible for the Section 538 program include individuals, partnerships, limited liability companies, and for-profit corporations. The rent and tenant eligibility criteria are similar to those of the Section 8 housing voucher program.

See **www.rurdev.usda.gov** for additional information.

State, County, Local, and Community-Based Programs

The availability of more local types of programs for assistance with property repair and improvement costs varies from state to state. For example, in Arizona, it is possible to find community home-repair assistance programs, in Maryland, the Department of Housing and Community Development has an indoor plumbing assistance program and a lead-hazard reduction grant and loan program, and in Indiana, the state Housing and Community Development department administers a homeowner-occupied rehabilitation program.

See **www.hud.gov** for links to all the states, which in turn link to the various programs that are available for the purchase and rehabilitation of residential property.

11

MOBILE HOMES AND MOBILE-HOME PARKS

As the costs of buying, owning, and financing a house and of renting an apartment continue to rise, mobile homes are the affordable housing option for many individuals. Improved manufacturing techniques and low utility bills make mobile homes attractive to low- and middle-income people, the elderly, and others who cannot afford or do not want conventional housing.

Note: Although not technically accurate, the term "mobile home" is used throughout this book for purposes of brevity and familiarity. The actual definition of "mobile home" is a dwelling unit built in a factory before June 15, 1976.

For reasons that will be noted below, investors in mobile homes often find that the next logical step in their investment careers is to buy the land on which mobile homes are located. This can be a small piece of private land, or it can be a mobile-home park where other units are located.

Essentially, an investor in mobile homes or mobile-home parks makes money in much the same way that an investor in multiunit residential property does: by leveraging, that is, by using a small amount of cash to generate a good rate of return.

As mentioned in Chapter 1, investing in mobile homes is different from investing in multiunit rental properties and other forms of real estate because a mobile home is "personalty," which is legal parlance for personal property. In contrast, the purchase of a mobile-home park involves real estate and, frequently, existing mobile homes. In such a case, the transaction is a hybrid sale and purchase of real estate and personal property.

The Changed Face of Mobile Homes

The mobile homes of today are not the rickety trailers of yesterday. Mobile homes now are built on foundations, and they come with many attractive features. Upscale mobile homes may come with amenities such as whirlpool baths; stainless steel sinks; high-quality, name-brand appliances; and even fireplaces.

What the average person commonly refers to as a "mobile home" is now more likely to be a "manufactured home," depending on when the unit was built. A manufactured home is defined as a single-family house that is constructed in the controlled environment of a factory and built in accordance with the Federal Manufactured Home Construction and Safety Standards, which is the only national building code that exists in the United States. Because the standards are administered by the Department of Housing and Urban Development, they are known collectively as the HUD Code.

There are several types of factory-built housing:

- **Mobile homes.** Technically, this term now refers to units that were manufactured before the June 15, 1976, effective date of the HUD Code.

- **Manufactured homes.** These may consist of one piece or several pieces that are transported to a site, assembled, and installed. The HUD Code regulates the design and construction of manufactured homes, as well as their strength, durability, transportability, energy efficiency, and fire resistance. Additionally, the HUD Code dictates the performance standards of the electrical, plumbing, air-conditioning, and thermal systems of manufactured homes.

- **Modular homes.** These are homes built in accordance with the state, local, or regional code that applies in the place where the home will be situated. A modular home is transported from the factory and installed on site.

- **Panelized homes.** For this type of home, panels consisting of entire walls with doors, windows, wiring, and exterior siding are transported to and assembled on the site.

- **Pre-cut homes.** The building materials for this type of home are factory-cut to design specifications before being transported to and assembled on the site. State or local building codes govern.

Modular Homes and Manufactured Homes

Modular homes are built on temporary metal frames. After the modular home is set on a foundation, the temporary frame is removed. In contrast, federal law prohibits the removal of the metal frame from a manufactured home. At any rate, if the frame of a manufactured home were removed, the weight of the unit would cause damage to the floor framing system.

Manufactured homes have a red, aluminum HUD label attached near the rear tail light. An identification number is stamped on the label. Modular homes do not have HUD labels.

Single-Wides and Double-Wides

Because of a housing shortage in the United States after World War II, many itinerant workers and members of the military began living in towable trailers. Within a few years, young families with children had become the predominant occupants of trailer homes. As an increasing number of people began living in trailers year-round, they began to care less about mobility and more about having units with additional room and a closer resemblance to houses.

Originally, state law governed the size of towable trailers, and the laws differed from state to state. Nonetheless, most states limited the trailers to a maximum of 35 feet long, 8 feet wide, and 12.5 feet high.

The mid-1950s saw the introduction of a unit that was wider than it was long and that was more a home than a vehicle. Dubbed a "mobile home," this new unit was 10 feet wide and was internally subdivided into discrete spaces. The "10-wide" could not be towed by car and instead was designed to be set down permanently on a site.

By 1969, manufacturers were making 14-foot wide mobile homes. The architectural designs and materials of these "single-wides" were more varied than those of the 10-wides. The new single-wides also offered more optional features, such as walk-in closets and cathedral ceilings.

Manufacturers also began producing "double-wides," which are multi-sectional manufactured homes that are towed to a site and assembled there. Double-wides can have several bedrooms, and the upscale ones are luxurious. There are even two-story designs and models with garages and breezeways. Many people who possess just a passing acquaintance with manufactured housing find it difficult to distinguish the double-wide of today from a "stick-built" ranch-style house.

Advantages of Investing in Mobile Homes

In the past 20 years, there has been a surge of interest in real estate investment. But there are far fewer competitors in the area of mobile home investment. The lack of competitors makes it likelier that an investor will be able to find viable opportunities and to buy what he or she wants, instead of settling for a second or third choice.

If an investor wants to start "small," he or she does not need much money to buy a mobile home. By renting the land on which the mobile home is situated, the investor saves tens of thousands of dollars on the purchase price. Because the purchase price is lower, the down payment and the payments on the note will be substantially lower as well. It costs no more, and frequently less, to buy a brand-new manufactured home than it does to buy an older house that is a fixer-upper.

One of the preferred ways in which investors in mobile homes turn a profit is by purchasing units from previous owners. These investors are also always on the lookout for repossessed units. Lenders can be a source of repossessed mobile homes, and savvy investors are able to convince dealers to sell them several such units at one time at wholesale prices. By buying previously owned or repossessed mobile homes, investors may find, for example, that they can pay as little as $15,000 for units that went for $60,000 brand new just two years earlier.

The owner of a mobile home that sits on land belonging to someone else does not pay real property taxes. Another advantage for the investor is that a mobile home is easier to maintain and less expensive to repair than a traditional house. An owner with minimal skills often can do the repairs, if he or she so chooses.

The main benefit for an investor in mobile homes is the cash flow that can be generated. According to experienced investors, the trick to this is to buy a unit inexpensively and then quickly sell it on a note that the investor takes back.

Some investors report that they concentrate on lower-income mobile-home parks, where they look for units that the owners, not other investors, are trying to sell. These investors claim that they frequently can buy units for less than $3,000. If the lot rental is $200 per month and an investor can put in a person who pays $500 per month for a specific number of years to purchase the unit, a positive cash flow of $300 per month is created.

Additionally, because the person in the unit is buying it, his or her contract with the investor will specify that the buyer is responsible for the maintenance costs. Thus, the holder of a note does not make repairs to the mobile home and instead only has to wait for the monthly payments to arrive.

If the buyer defaults on the note, the mobile home goes back to the investor, who can again arrange for its purchase and again receive a positive cash flow each month. It is not uncommon to sell, take back, and resell a mobile home repeatedly. This is why renowned investor Lonnie Scruggs has called the mobile home "the perpetual money machine."

After a while, an investor who operates in a particular area will become known by lenders, mobile-home park managers, and even mobile home parts suppliers. Those sources will prove valuable as they begin referring to the investor people who are interested in buying or selling a unit.

Longtime investors are able to buy and sell mobile homes with no cash outlay of their own. They do this by agreeing to buy a used mobile home for a low price and simultaneously lining up someone to buy the unit from them. For example, Al agrees to buy a single-wide home from Bruce for $500. Al is allowed to put a "For Sale" sign in the window of the unit.

Al then gets a call from Carrie, who needs a place as soon as possible and is willing to pay $4,500 plus taxes and fees of $1,000. Carrie pays Al a $1,500 down payment, from which Al pays Bruce $500. Al takes back a note from Carrie for $4,000 at 12 percent for 2 years. This amounts to $188.29 per month for 24 months for Al, who can turn around and sell the note to someone else.

Inspection of Used Mobile Homes

Before buying a used mobile home, an investor or someone with sufficient relevant experience must examine the unit carefully. This is the only way to determine the maximum to pay for a unit.

Some states allow dealers to sell mobile homes in any condition, whether they are ready for the scrap heap or have been completely rebuilt. Other states impose strict standards on used mobile homes sold by dealers.

Sometimes, dealers buy a quantity of mobile homes that have been through natural disasters and were sold by their owners to make room for replacement housing on their lots. Water or fire damage may be concealed by a fresh coat of paint, new paneling on the walls, new boards on the ceiling, or new carpeting.

Other signs of trouble to look for include:

- Metal roof that is too loose or wrinkled or that is stretched too tightly on a hot, sunny day

- Shingled roof with ridges or dips in the surface or that has broken, missing, or misaligned shingles

- Shingled roof with less than a 6-inch overhang

- Ceilings that sag or are cracked

- Wallboard panels that are broken or loose

- Vinyl siding that is attached tightly to the sheathing underneath or that is notably bowed, warped, or badly fitted around doors and windows

- Inferior-grade kitchen cabinets made of wall paneling on 1-inch by 1-inch framing

- Metal siding torn or wrinkled at the screw hole locations

- Metal frame that sags over the wheel

- Bottom board material (black plastic sheeting) with large holes

- Inadequate insulation in the walls, roof, and under the floor

- Undersized 20-gallon water heater

- Tub and shower compartments with shower walls made with Sheetrock covered with vinyl or cellulose wallboard and batten trim over the corner joints

This list is far from exhaustive. Investors are cautioned to become familiar with the types of defects that are common with mobile homes, either on their own or with the help of experts.

The Purchase Contract

"Because a mobile home is considered by law to be personal property, its sale comes under the Uniform Commercial Code (UCC) regulations," explains attorney Estelle Flynn Lord. The UCC is a model set of laws that govern the sale of products, and it has been adopted in all 50 states.

As a result, if a buyer uses financing for all or part of the purchase price of a mobile home, there will be a note for the amount financed. To secure his or her interest, the seller will file a UCC lien in the state and county where the mobile home is located. In this sense, the UCC lien functions in a manner similar to a mortgage, which secures a loan for the purchase of real estate. With a UCC lien, the seller can get back the mobile home if the buyer fails to keep up with the payments on the note.

Flynn Lord cautioned, "Because the UCC and its regulations may not be what you consider to be normal or logical, it is important for the parties to be represented by attorneys who are familiar with the intricacies of the statute and regulations." She added, "The attorneys will have to scrutinize the language of the parties' contract, which may be deceptively similar to that used for the purchase and sale of real estate. The law treats the contracts in very different ways."

When buying a mobile home from a dealer, the investor should carefully read the front and back of all the pages of the purchase agreement. The cost of delivery and installation will be included in the price of the mobile home, but the back of the agreement will likely state that the buyer will pay for a bulldozer or wrecker, if needed, to place the unit on site. If there are any questions about this, before signing the agreement, an investor may insist that the dealer send someone competent to the proposed site to determine whether the mobile home being purchased can be placed at the site and whether a bulldozer or wrecker will be necessary.

Mobile-Home Parks

Mobile-home parks come in a wide variety of sizes, layouts, and management styles. Parks with up to 20 mobile homes may be informal, with few facilities, no paved streets, and no set scheme for the placement of the units. As a result, the mobile homes in such parks tend to be set down haphazardly, often cramped together on tiny plots. In contrast, parks with 50 or more mobile homes commonly adhere to a site plan and offer more structure. These larger parks have rules in place, thus showing that someone is in control.

There are upscale mobile-home parks that cater to the retired, and there are poorly run, strictly utilitarian parks that attract low-income individuals and the occasional undesirable element. As in the old days of trailer parks, these downscale mobile-home parks can be found near construction sites and meat-packing plants, in rural localities where migrant workers need cheap housing, and near military bases. They also serve as emergency housing in areas where disaster has struck.

Most of the smaller mobile-home parks are managed by an individual owner. Larger parks are frequently owned by mobile-home dealers or manufacturers, national chains, or institutional investors, and many of them have on-site, full-time managers.

Complicated building and zoning regulations have discouraged the development of mobile-home parks in urban areas, although ironically, this is where inexpensive housing is most needed. Compliance with those regulations can be an expensive, drawn-out process. Many municipalities do not want mobile-home parks within their limits and therefore do not plan for them. This makes it difficult to find suitable land for new mobile-home parks, even on the outskirts of town.

On the other hand, in Florida and throughout the South and the West, living in a mobile home does not carry the stigma that it does in other parts of the country. Many places in those areas have witnessed the growth of upscale mobile-home parks near golf courses and marinas. The layout of these parks is like a subdivision of residential houses in the suburbs. Some of the parks provide a sense of safety to the residents with 24-hour security. The lawns are maintained, and the paved streets are well lit and helpfully signed. Many parks have clubhouses with restaurants and convenience stores, and there may be a heated swimming pool and a tennis court, just to name a few amenities. No cramped groupings here: the double-wides sit on lots spacious enough for two-car parking and patios. There are also many opportunities for the residents to socialize at club meetings, dances, classes, and tournaments. The developers of these mobile-home parks frequently market them as "resorts" or "communities."

CASE STUDY: DAVID REYNOLDS

MHP Investment and Leasing, LLC
P.O. Box 457
Cedar Edge, CO 81413
(800) 304-2835
www.mobilehomeparkstore.com

I invest primarily in mobile-home parks in different states, with particular focus in the Midwest and coastal areas; I am also a certified public accountant. Overall I think mobile-home parks are thriving more than many other types of real estate because mobile homes are affordable housing. The cap rates, cash-on-cash returns, and other numbers are much better on mobile-home parks than on apartment buildings, self-storage facilities, and other niche investments.

I started my Web site, **www.mobilehomeparkstore.com**, about 10 years ago as a place for brokers and individuals to list mobile-home parks for sale. The site has grown to about 4,000 pages that feature financing companies, insurance companies, and all the other supporting industries that offer solutions to virtually any problem faced by investors. I have also written books with another investor, Frank Rolse, on the different aspects of investing in parks. The books are available through my Web site and others.

To familiarize myself with areas in which I may want to buy a park, I initially look at **www.city-data.com** and **www.bestplaces.net** for demographics. I also research the other parks in the area, apartment rents, and other factors. Real estate agents are always looking out for parks that might fit the criteria that I require; mostly I use my Web site and a few others to find parks.

CASE STUDY: DAVID REYNOLDS

My advice to those considering investing in mobile-home parks is: (1) learn as much as you can, go to the forums, and read articles and other materials, (2) when you find a park that looks like something you want to buy, do complete and thorough due diligence so that you do not make a big mistake, and (3) do not put much value on or pay extra for vacant lots because in this market they are hard to fill.

Benefits of Owning a Mobile-Home Park

When an investor buys land with the mobile homes that are on it, he or she is buying real estate and personal property, and the transaction will involve both types of purchases. In other words, not only will a deed to the land pass to the buyer, the seller will file a UCC lien if financing for the mobile homes is involved.

There are relatively fewer people interested in investing in mobile homes with land than there are buyers of mobile homes. As for the purchase price, not only is it less expensive to buy a mobile home with land than it is to buy a traditional house on land, experienced investors have reported that they can often pay the same amount of money for a mobile home with land that they would spend for a mobile home on someone else's land (for which rent must be paid). The reason for this is that a mobile-home park is frequently located in an unfavorable part of a town, which makes the land inexpensive. Additionally, the cost of the land will be spread over several mobile homes because, whether they own or rent, the occupants will be paying to rent the land on which their mobile homes sit.

David Reynolds buys mobile-home parks throughout the United States. He began by investing in mobile homes 13 years ago.

"When I started, I did almost everything. I was buying mobile homes, fixing them up, and selling them. I bought them in other people's parks, some of them in my own parks. I would buy a home for $3,000 or $4,000 and then sell it for $8,000 or $9,000 on a contract. That would work real well in some markets, but then there would be repossessions, and I would have to go back in and spend $3,000 or $4,000 more to fix up a home and sell it again. The only benefit I ever had from that was when I was buying and putting them in my own park, because then I was getting the lot rent in perpetuity."

Another key benefit for the investor is that the value of the land that is bought along with a mobile home should appreciate over time. Equity in the land also will grow with the pay down of the loans used to finance the purchase.

Some investors may find that it is more beneficial, in terms of cash flow and tax benefits, to rent out mobile homes with land than it is to buy and then sell the mobile homes on the land. The tenant pays for living in the mobile home, in addition to the land on which it sits, and the value of the mobile home itself can be depreciated. Later, when the investor no longer wants the role of landlord, he or she can sell the mobile home and keep collecting rent for the land.

If the owner of a mobile home wants to move out of a park, he or she will find that the fees for state licenses and the restrictions on the transportation of oversized loads on state roadways make the movement of the mobile home impractical. As a result, the owner is more likely to buy a mobile home at a new location and sell the old one, either to the park or to a third party. For the owner of the mobile-home park, this creates a real opportunity to get the pre-owned mobile home for a bargain price.

John Hyre is a tax attorney in Ohio who is gradually building his inventory of mobile-home parks. He said, "If you can buy a park with rental homes in it cheaply, there is a great opportunity to turn it around by selling the homes." Hyre added, "The problem is that often, the sellers value the homes for much more than they are worth."

The ownership of a mobile-home park also makes it easier to replace outdated mobile homes with newer models that meet the needs of the market than when a mobile home is in a mobile-home park that belongs to another person. The investor can keep the cost of upgrades down by buying used or repossessed mobile homes of more recent vintage. In addition, the owner of a mobile-home park who is trying to upgrade the park has the right to refuse to rent land for units that exceed a specific age.

Hyre is an example of an investor who saw opportunity in a poorly run and maintained mobile-home park.

"The more lots the owner rented out, the more money he would lose. He was charging $200 per month for lot rent, which was about right for that area, but he was paying more than that per lot in variable costs. The primary reason was water. The owner was getting hammered three different ways on water. First, the small town this park is in disliked him and was charging him commercial rates for water. Second, he did not submeter the water, which really hurt him; his tenants would have their friends come over to wash their cars. Third, the infrastructure below ground was old, and there were many leaks. So the first thing we did was change the water pipes and submeter at the same time. That turned the park from a massive money-loser into about breaking even almost immediately."

Hyre and his partner took additional steps to turn the park around.

"When we bought the park, there were no rules; there were many junk, rusted-out homes; and several really nasty people in there. One of the rules that we set that has been helpful is that if the police visit you twice, you are gone. It works, and the cops and the town love us for it. We also do not tolerate any junk in the yard, jacked up cars, and the like. Another rule that makes a massive difference is that we grandfathered the mobile homes that were in there. We might require some painting or vinyl skirting, but we do not make people vinyl-side them. But as soon as the home is sold and someone new moves in, we require siding. This has made a tremendous difference in the look of the park. We also paved where there used to be what I would call a moonscape of gravel. Between putting in the black asphalt with the nice yellow lines, cleaning things up, and forcing the vinyl siding and skirting, the look of the park has improved immeasurably. People are willing to move in, given the good prices for the homes and the fact that we got rid of the troublemakers."

By owning the land on which a mobile home sits, the owner may resort to the eviction provisions of state landlord/tenant laws. Evictions of nonpaying tenants are simpler and faster than repossessions of mobile homes for nonpayment under a note.

Most important, an investor in mobile homes with land is able to take advantage of leverage. Thus, instead of buying an older mobile home in a park that belongs to someone else, the investor can use that same money and leverage it with loans to buy a mobile-home park with mobile homes on it. In this way, the investor ends up with a property of greater value for the same amount of money.

According to experienced investors, lenders understand real estate investments better than they do mobile-home investments. As in a traditional real estate setting, a lender can use appraisals, comparable sales, and tax assessments to confirm the value of the land on which a mobile home sits.

Another potential benefit is that a park that is at least 20 percent vacant at the time of purchase presents the new owner with the opportunity to make improvements, add amenities, raise the rents, and bring in additional mobile homes — all to increase the rent roll. Each of these steps instantly increases the value of the park by enhancing its cap rate valuation, which is a method of determining the value of commercial property. The cap rate, or capitalization rate, is the ratio of net operating income to the purchase price. The net operating income (NOI) is the income after payment of all the expenses except the loans on the property, the taxes, and the recovery of capital.

To see how to determine the cap rate, assume that a mobile-home park in Myrtle Beach, South Carolina, is priced at $300,000 and that its annual net operating income is $25,000:

$$\$25,000 \text{ (NOI)} \div \$300,000 \text{ (purchase price)} = .83 \text{ (8.3 percent) cap rate}$$

By knowing the average cap rate in the area in which a mobile-home park is located, an investor can determine whether the cap rate of the park is above or below average. The higher the cap rate sought by the investor, the lower the price that he or she is willing to pay for the property. Conversely, the seller prefers a cap rate that is lower than the average because this will allow a higher price for the property.

After buying a mobile-home park, the new owner may find that the cash flow is unsatisfactory. The owner can create additional revenue streams by providing conveniences such as coin-operated laundries, vending machines, lawn-care service, self-storage facilities, and even day care service.

If the new owner buys mobile homes at a deep discount, such as 40 to 50 percent, or even wholesale directly from a manufacturer, and then sells the units for market price rather than renting them, several advantages are gained.

- The owner, at no extra cost, will be receiving lot rents

- The owner will have people in the park who will take pride in their homes and who are more likely than renters to take care of them

- The buyers of the mobile homes will be solely responsible for their upkeep

- If a buyer fails to keep up with payments on the note, the park owner, as the one who financed the deal, will be able to take back the mobile home and resell it, all while keeping the original down payment, the payments on the note, and the benefit of any repairs or upgrades made by the defaulting buyer

Renting Out Recreational Facilities

If you have or will put up in your mobile-home park a facility for recreational use by the residents, you may consider renting it out for a few hours at a time for special occasions, such as private parties or meetings. You will want a sufficiently large deposit and a flat rate for the period of the rental, with an additional hourly fee in case the function runs beyond the specified period.

Another crucial issue is insurance. Your insurance for the park may not cover private functions. Even if it does, it is prudent to require whoever is renting the facility to obtain short-term special event insurance. Along these same lines, you will want a "hold harmless" provision in the rental agreement that makes the renter entirely responsible in case of a liability, such as a slip and fall, and that requires the renter to indemnify you in case you are held liable.

Financing the Purchase

Investing in mobile-home parks does not have to involve large sums of up-front cash. Many are bought with less than the 20 percent down payment that a commercial lender would require, and seller financing is frequently used for the balance of the purchase price. Many mobile-home park owners who offer financing to buyers seek the benefit of putting off payment of the capital gains tax.

Many "mom-and-pop owners" who have been operating small to medium-size mobile-home parks for a long time tend to have many vacancies in their parks. This is due to the overabundance of repossessed mobile homes that flooded the market after a meltdown in the mobile-home industry in the late 1990s. The glut of mobile homes on the market, in addition to the corresponding vacancies in the parks, has made it difficult for park owners to refinance or sell the parks in a conventional manner. On the other hand, this situation is a boon to investors who seek high-quality, inexpensive mobile homes today.

One way that an investor can reduce his or her risk and the amount of cash outlay is by negotiating a lease with an option to purchase a mobile-home park. For example, the lease may be for a term of seven years, after which the option to purchase could be exercised. For the owner of a park that has not generated ROI for some time and that is running in the red, a lease with an option to purchase may be ideal. The owner will be relieved of managing the park and making up the monthly cash-flow shortfall to cover the operating expenses, while gaining the benefit of deferring the capital gains tax on the amount received for the option, which becomes part of the sales price only when the option is exercised.

Investor David Reynolds said he sees little difficulty in obtaining financing these days from conventional lenders.

"Twenty years ago, it was extremely hard to find financing for a mobile-home park. They were not understood by lenders, and everyone had a horrible image of what they were. Then lenders started figuring out that several of the guys who were buying mobile home parks were on the Forbes 400 list. There were several big players out there, and for the banks, it was a matter of 'we have to get into this' because the foreclosure rate is lower, and they liked it. As far as the credit crunch goes, a couple of lenders have pulled out because of some of the loans they made in the past involving many park-owned homes, but it is still relatively easy to find loans and loan programs. The rates are about the same as before the crunch. The only thing that has changed is that lenders like to see a little more down payment. A year ago, you possibly could find 15 to 20 percent down; now it is 20 to 25 percent."

As revealed in Chapter 7, the FHA has a loan program for the financing of mobile homes that will be situated on land owned by the purchaser and a loan program for mobile homes in mobile-home parks owned by others. Yet, experts in mobile home and mobile-home park investing have indicated that it may be difficult to find lenders that offer these FHA loans. These experts advise investors to look to small banks as sources of the FHA loans or to ask mobile-home dealers where to obtain such financing. According to some seasoned investors, the key to qualifying for an FHA loan is to obtain a certification from an engineer that the foundation system for the manufactured home complies with the HUD Code requirements; doing so may necessitate the installation of a steel foundation.

The availability of different kinds of government-backed financing varies from state to state. A mortgage broker should be able to help locate lenders that administer those types of programs.

Challenges

Unlike duplexes, triplexes, and fourplexes, mobile homes and mobile-home parks present a number of unique challenges to investors.

Zoning

Local governments have specific zoning regulations that deal with the location of mobile-home parks. According to attorney Estelle Flynn Lord, some places discourage mobile-home parks out of concern about attracting transients. Many municipalities effectively banish mobile-home parks to the fringes of town or to isolated areas. Although this location can mean lower prices for an investor, it also means that plans to expand or even upgrade a park may never come to fruition because obtaining the necessary approvals and permits would be difficult, if not impossible.

Insurance

Insuring mobile homes is a highly specialized field that many insurance companies will not touch. Insurers abhor risk, and they consider mobile homes highly risky because of the threats posed by severe weather and fires.

Nonetheless, some insurance companies will take on the risk of insuring mobile homes. They can be found by speaking with mobile-home dealers, lenders, real estate agents, and even the seller. There are also Web sites for mobile home investors that offer information on insurance and other matters.

As for insuring mobile-home parks, investors David Reynolds and John Hyre report no difficulties in obtaining coverage. According to Reynolds:

"There are quite a few great insurance programs out there. The biggest problem is in Florida and some coastal areas that had the hurricanes. Insurance is a little bit higher in those areas. But you really just own the dirt, the actual land, so you are not insuring structures. The liability insurance for the park is practically available everywhere."

Hyre also has obtained insurance readily. He noted:

"If you run a park correctly, you can really reduce the liability because you are not dealing with mechanicals like you would be in a regular unit — no furnace issues, toilet issues, especially if you rehab the plumbing the way we did; physically, you should not have issues. Now as to what the residents do, you have to be all over them. They create the liability."

Hyre also has this advice about insurance coverage:

"I tell my clients when we discuss asset protection to be aware of the exclusions. For example, if we move a mobile home into our park, the policy for the park will not cover an accident involved in the moving of the home. So you have to make sure your mover is insured, and you cannot take his word for it. You need an insurance certificate from an insurance company directly. You are going to pay extra for that quality of mover, but it is worth it. We kicked a client out over this. We inspected a home and approved it to be moved in but told him that we had to approve the mover. He just went ahead and got a farmer buddy who dragged the home in on a tractor. The farmer ran over a gas main, the entire park had to be evacuated, and the fire department came in. This did not help us with community relations. The farmer thankfully did not cause any damage other than run over someone's yard and leave tire tracks."

Licensing

Some states, such as California and Texas, require anyone who sells more than a few mobile homes on notes per year to obtain a dealer's license. Investors who plan to buy and sell mobile homes will need to check the laws in their states for the threshold of activity that triggers the requirement of a dealer's license.

"Flipping" Mobile Homes

The investor who tries to flip a mobile home strictly to raise cash will find that potential buyers will have a hard time finding affordable financing from a conventional lender. The lender will likely insist on a 20 percent down payment and a double-digit interest rate.

For a possible solution, many seasoned investors suggest that small community banks are more willing to provide financing to buyers of mobile homes.

Upkeep and Emergency Repairs

An emergency repair can wipe out several months' worth of cash flow from a mobile-home park. For example, an investor may have to repair a ruptured water line or sewer pipe.

If the park is old, it may not be fitted with a sewer system and instead may have a septic system in place. The septic system will need to be cleaned out periodically by a professional and replaced if the number of park occupants grows larger than the system can support.

The key to dealing with the unexpected is to include a financial cushion in the investment plan. The investor must be able to take care of emergency repairs or disruptions in cash flow caused by disappearing tenants. This is why it is not a good idea for an investor to sink all his or her money into the purchase and upgrade of a mobile-home park.

The Future

There are divergent outlooks on the future of mobile homes and mobile-home parks. Some investors believe that rising interest rates and the rising costs of traditional home ownership will drive more individuals into buying or renting mobile homes and living in mobile-home parks.

As evidence of the continuing viability of this type of investment, many cite the fact that prolific investor Warren Buffett bought a portfolio of mobile-home parks for $1.7 billion in 2003. In a letter to his shareholders that year, Buffet even declared that manufactured homes "can deliver very good value" to investors. He also noted in the letter that for decades, 15 percent of the homes built in the United States have been manufactured homes.

Many experts expect the demand for mobile homes to remain healthy, particularly among people in the lower- or middle-income brackets who always need affordable housing options. Relatively few affordable homes exist or are being built in the United States. Mobile homes themselves have been increasing in price, and the scarcity of conventional financing makes owner financing with affordable payments particularly attractive to those who cannot otherwise buy a mobile home. The notes on such deals, in turn, are attractive to the investor because of the high yields and cash flow they produce.

Investor David Reynolds sees positive changes in attitudes toward mobile-home parks.

"Ten years ago, most cities did not like mobile-home parks at all. You can see that is changing a little bit now because they know that mobile homes really are the best affordable housing for their people. Many parks have been closing over the past five to ten years, and now you see cities trying to retain their parks and keep them updated and cleaned up so they are not an eyesore but a good alternative for lower-income people."

On the other hand, in some areas, investors in mobile homes have reported having trouble finding qualified buyers for their units. The carrying costs for some investors in this situation have been so high that they have had to sell low, sometimes at a loss, or have had the units cut up and hauled away so that they do not have to continue making lot-rental payments.

CASE STUDY: JOHN HYRE, ESQ.

870 High St, Suite 104
Worthington, OH 43085
(614) 207-2441
www.realestatetaxlaw.com
johnhyre@ameritech.com

I am a tax attorney who caters only to real estate investors. Mobile homes and mobile-home parks are my sideline, and they help build wealth over time. I began investing in mobile homes in 1999. In 2001, a partner and I bought four mobile homes with land, which is a "park" under Ohio law. In 2006 we bought a 22-unit park in Indiana, where the law is much more favorable. We are looking for more 10- to 50-unit parks in Indiana within easy driving distance from Ohio with the goal of getting enough units so that we can centralize management.

I began investing in mobile homes because I liked the low startup costs; between purchase and rehabilitation I think I paid on average $3,000 for a mobile home. There is also comparatively low risk. I also started off as a nice guy, but dealing with tenants will knock that out of you quickly; otherwise, you will go broke.

I learned that renting out mobile homes is not a good idea, at least above the Mason-Dixon line, where the culture is not friendly toward mobile homes. Also, the liability and aggravation of dealing with renters were not worth the trouble. The large institutional investors are not interested in parks with fewer than 100 lots. The cap rates on the smaller parks are much higher and it's much easier to get a bargain. We genuinely like our niche.

My advice to those interested in investing in mobile-home parks is: (1) strong due diligence, (2) if the cash flow for a park that is for sale includes mobile-home rents, either exclude them or discount extraordinarily deeply when calculating the value of the park, and (3) sell the mobile homes in your park on payments; this reduces your liability and maintenance and gives the residents a sense of ownership.

12

EFFECTIVE NEGOTIATION

After a closing has taken place, title has passed, and everyone has been paid, the investor alone must live with the deal he or she has made. To have no regrets, the investor must make sure at each stage leading to the closing that he or she has negotiated the best terms possible, whether the transaction is a purchase or a sale.

In the real estate field, investors, attorneys, real estate agents, and other professionals who are active in a given locality tend to know or at least have heard of each other. This is why it is advisable for you as an investor to maintain good relations with those you meet, to treat them with respect, and to develop a reputation for honesty and fairness. In the close-knit world of real estate, your reputation — good or bad — as someone with whom to do business will precede you. Your negotiation style will be a key component of your reputation.

Instead of depending on luck to find good deals, an investor can learn to hammer out good deals. This chapter describes negotiation tactics and strategies that can help you get the deal you want when buying or selling a property without coming across as overaggressive and arrogant. Many of these approaches will also work in negotiations with tenants, contractors, lenders, government agencies, and others.

Superior Knowledge

If you know more about a property than anyone else (even the seller), you stand a superior chance of successfully negotiating the terms of a transaction involving the property. By creating your investment plan, researching your target area and state and local laws, and performing your precontract and postcontract due diligence, you, as a buyer, will know the maximum price that you should pay for a property. As a seller, you will need to have a realistic idea of the value of your rental property based on factors such as the current supply and demand for properties such as yours in the marketplace.

You do not want to find yourself in negotiations with a party who enjoys a superior bargaining position based on having more knowledge about a property than you. You will recognize that this has happened when the other party readily accepts your first offer.

You must at least have information that is comparable to that possessed by the other party. The use of experts, such as a property inspector, an insurance agent, and an attorney, will help level the playing field, but you cannot dispense with your own preliminary research. It is only when you are armed with information of good quality that you can intelligently anticipate the terms that the other party will accept or reject; the ability to anticipate the thoughts and strategies of the other party is what puts you in control of a deal.

People Skills

The key to a successful encounter with other people is to put them at ease. This is also the point of being courteous, which you should strive to be throughout a transaction. To get a meaningful negotiation going, you will want to say things that elicit a positive response from the other person and that encourage him or her to prolong the discussion, not cut it off brusquely.

You do not want to come off as intimidating; you also should not be patronizing to the other person or try to humiliate him or her. Ask questions and actively listen to the answers — do not just wait for your turn to speak. By listening carefully, you can pick up clues on how to word your offers and counteroffers.

You must not complain; it is off-putting and does not win sympathy. You should aim to appear as a leader who is in control, well-informed, and well-organized. You should also know when not to speak.

Above all else, keep emotions out of the deal. Successful negotiators, whether in real estate investment or other fields, avoid jeopardizing their bargaining position and their chance of getting the terms they want by not allowing their emotions to build to the point that their control of the deal evaporates.

If you can find a way to connect with a seller, he or she is more likely to want to deal with you and less likely to accept a better offer from another person who fails to establish a rapport.

Changes Backed by Reasons

If you want to negotiate changes in terms or conditions of a purchase and sale contract, you will need to have solid reasons for your requests. Perhaps you are looking for a $5,000 reduction in the sales price because that is how much it will cost you to replace a furnace on which the seller delayed maintenance for years. You must inform the seller of your reasoning so that it does not seem that you are looking to reduce the price by an arbitrary amount.

As another example, it could be that your property inspector found outdated knob-and-tube electrical wiring in a house, and you know from your insurance agent that you would have to try to obtain insurance for the property from the residual market, which will mean substantially higher rates than those offered by a preferred insurer. In that case, you must let the seller know in no uncertain terms that you cannot buy the property as is because it is effectively uninsurable. If the deal is to be saved, the seller will have to pay to have the electrical wiring updated, give you a discount on the purchase price to reflect the property as is, or "give back" money to you at closing in the form of a credit so that you can take care of the electrical upgrade. If the seller balks at these choices, you will need to point out that any subsequent buyer will run into the same insurance problem; the seller would then have to decide whether to deal with the electrical condition now or later.

Negotiation Tactics & Techniques

When a buyer faces the prospect of paying more than he or she wants for a property, the buyer should express a willingness to pay the asking price if the seller is willing to accept the terms of the buyer. This allows the seller to feel successful about making the buyer meet the asking price and gives the buyer the satisfaction of knowing that he or she obtained the terms that made the deal feasible. On the other hand, if the seller is playing the "there are plenty of other buyers out there" card, the buyer can call the seller's bluff by presenting a lower offer on a "take it or leave it" basis. Nonetheless, because of the finality of the "take it or leave it" position, many negotiators adopt it only as a last resort.

Some of the tactics for use in the negotiation of a real estate contract include:

"Soft" Letters of Intent

Letters of intent are used in all forms of real estate except single-family properties, which go directly to contracts for purchase and sale. A letter of intent allows a buyer and a seller to negotiate many of the essential terms of the sale — such as the price and the amount of time to close — between themselves before their lawyers become involved. A soft letter of intent takes a person-to-person approach by starting out with a compliment to the seller, a mention of a common tie between the buyer and the seller, and a brief explanation of why the buyer is interested in the property. The letter also can include a ballpark figure of what the buyer believes to be a fair price, and it ends with an invitation to the seller for further discussion. To write this type of letter, a buyer must find out details about the seller, such as extracurricular activities and club or organization memberships, and about the property.

Option Contracts

An option contract allows the buyer to tie up a property for little cash and to "soften" the purchase price. An option contract is best used when a buyer already knows that he or she wants to buy a property and will close on it if the seller grants the buyer the time he or she has requested. For example, if the buyer needs time to bring other investors into a deal, he or she may offer a few thousand dollars as an option payment to the seller, with the understanding that if other investors are not found in six months, the seller will keep the money and be free to sell the property to someone else.

Floating Seller-Held Mortgages

When it is apparent during negotiations that the seller is willing to act as the primary lender, the buyer should try to have the seller-held mortgage drafted in a way that allows the buyer to substitute another property as the security for the mortgage on the purchased property; this allows the buyer to sell the purchased property at a later time, without the need to pay off the mortgage or have the replacement buyer assume the mortgage. For example, Barbara purchases a triplex from Sam for $300,000 and obtains a conventional first mortgage for $200,000. Sam agrees to take back a note and second mortgage for $100,000 to be amortized in 15 years. The proper clause in the parties' contract will allow Barbara to "float" the second mortgage to a substitute property. The substitute property can be a property that Barbara currently owns or will buy later, another property owned by Barbara, or a property owned by another person (as long as that person agrees to the added obligation).

There are many other tactics and tools for successful negotiations. These include the use of contingency clauses in contracts and the insertion of a clause that grants the purchaser the sole right to extend the closing date under specific circumstances.

Saving Face

In the course of tough negotiations, you may arrive at a point where the other party feels backed against a wall. The fight or flight instinct will kick in, and the other party will either try aggressive tactics to get his or her own way or threaten to kill the deal. Even if you are in a superior bargaining position and the other party knows it, you will both drown in hostility, and the talks will stall if you do not throw out a lifeline to the other party. The way to do this is by allowing the other party to save face. This is a highly effective technique rooted in human psychology: no one likes to feel like the loser in a competitive setting. Therefore, in all negotiations, you must find a way to create a win-win situation.

The following example will demonstrate that the lifeline you throw to the other party can be slender. Let us assume that Jones LLC is at a closing to finalize the purchase of a 40-year-old duplex from Vick Vendor. In the pre-closing phase, Jones was able to negotiate numerous repairs to the old building from Vick. Now an issue has come up at the closing about termite damage that the property inspector had uncovered. Jones must present its lender with a certification from a pest inspection company that the damage has been remediated. Vick insists that he was never told about the termite damage and that he will not pay to fix the problem because Jones waived its right to demand corrective action.

Both parties know that Vick needs to take the funds from the sale to the closing on his new retirement home, which is scheduled for later that same day. Nonetheless, Vick digs in his heels because he resents what he sees as yet another concession being foisted on him. To move beyond this stalemate and to put the closing back on track, Jones needs to come up with a way for Vick to save face. Perhaps Vick had agreed to replace a washing machine in one of the units, and the appliance did not arrive by the closing date but will be delivered and installed the next day. Ordinarily, this delay would entitle Jones to escrow the amount of the washer and its installation until the installation was completed.

Instead, Jones tells Vick that it is confident that the washer will be delivered and installed as Vick has promised and that it is willing to waive the escrow for the washer if Vick agrees to grant a credit for remediation of the termite damage. Vick is likely to agree to this because (a) he knows that he failed to live up to his duty to have the washer installed by the date of closing, (b) Jones appears to be making a concession that it is not obligated to make, and (c) he is glad to find a way to complete the sale of the duplex and move on to the closing on his new home. For its part, Jones has nothing to lose because it has the receipt for the washer, and a one-day delay in the delivery and installation of the washer will not make a difference.

Every transaction will present opportunities to make small concessions in exchange for larger benefits. A smart investor views these opportunities as arrows in his or her quiver and the successful conclusion of a real estate transaction as the bull's-eye.

Work Together, Not Against Each Other

The most fruitful and least stressful negotiations occur when both sides realize that they are working together toward a common goal: the culmination of the transaction. In real life, this bilateral realization does not always occur.

Nevertheless, as someone who wants to be a successful negotiator, you must always keep your eyes on that goal. A seller may insist on a specific price. As long as the price is not out of line, you can agree to pay it, as long as the seller meets your other terms, such as paying for repairs, assisting with the closing costs, including extra appliances in the sale, or taking back financing. You can also insist on these types of terms if the seller wants to close more quickly or slowly than is usual.

Always Leave Wiggle Room

When you submit a contract to a seller, always ask for more than you expect to get. You may be surprised by what a seller is willing to give you. You will also give yourself room to make what appear to be concessions, and this will help give the seller the vital sense of being a winner.

No Splitting the Difference

Buyers should avoid offering to split the difference as a way to break a stalemate. Instead, the seller should be the one to propose splitting the difference, because this signals a willingness to accept a lower price. The buyer can then "reluctantly" offer to increase its price a little in exchange for a concession from the seller that is of greater value to the buyer. This is another face-saving technique.

Be Willing to Walk Away

This point has been made previously in this book, but it bears repeating. Keep your options open. Knowing what alternative properties are available will help keep you emotionally detached from the negotiation process, which, in turn, can be a powerful motivator to a seller to meet your terms and complete the transaction.

13

COMMON MISTAKES TO AVOID

The way to increase the chances of succeeding as an investor in duplexes, triplexes, fourplexes, mobile homes, and mobile-home parks is to reduce the exposure to risk. The principal way to reduce risk is by not committing avoidable mistakes.

There are many avoidable mistakes for the investor who is not prepared to act soberly and diligently. This chapter highlights some of the most common errors made by novice investors. Some of these errors are elaborated on in other chapters.

Ignoring the Calculator

The number one mistake made by would-be real estate investors is failing to carefully calculate the relevant numbers. A serious investor is one who has a vision of his or her future and who has set this vision down in an investment plan. This investor will not commit to spending money and time without first knowing how much he or she wants to spend, how much of a return he or she needs, and how long he or she will hold on to a property.

An investor who wants to succeed is also ready to analyze the income and the expenses — including the loan payments — involved with owning and operating a property.

Without this preparatory work, an investor is merely gambling that whatever he or she buys will somehow return a profit within an unspecified time.

Not Knowing Area Rents

When buying and holding property, the only way to know whether a property will produce sufficient income to satisfy the requirements of an investment plan is by being familiar with the amount of rent that is paid in a target area.

"It is crucial to ask around independently," cautioned attorney Estelle Flynn Lord.

In other words, an investor should not take the word of an owner, or even the word of a real estate agent, as to what rents to expect. The investor should check the rental listings in the local newspaper, ask other investors in similar properties in the targeted areas, and ask people who live and rent in the targeted areas.

Choosing an Inadequate Form of Ownership

The mistake of choosing an inadequate form of ownership can have severe consequences for the investor. As noted in Chapter 3, the investor should not jeopardize his or her personal assets while pursuing financial goals through investing in property. This is why it is too risky for an investor to buy rental property in his or her own name. Nonetheless, doing so may be appropriate if the investor plans to live in a unit of the purchased property or will otherwise receive favorable financing terms.

Other concerns that will play into the decision of which form of ownership to choose include the flexibility of the form, the tax consequences that apply, how long the property will be held after purchase, and the needs of the various partners involved in the venture.

Overpaying

Experience has long taught investors that they make their profit not when they sell a property, but when they buy it. This means not overpaying in the first place. The investor who overpays will be unable to make back as much as would have been possible had a lower price been negotiated. An investor cannot be sure that the next purchaser will help make up for that mistake because the next purchaser could be an experienced real estate investor who knows better than to overpay.

An investor may have to patiently wait out the market to get a good price. As Stephen DiClemente, a real estate agent in New Jersey, observed, many sellers continue to hold on to ideals that clash with the harsh reality of the times:

"Many sellers are not ready to drop their prices. In fact, I read that 67 percent of people in the country do not think that their homes devalued in 2007, even though the National Association of Realtors has said that prices were down 8 percent in the United States. People still think their houses have appreciated in value. They are not willing to bite the bullet. That is why only about 30 percent of homes actually sell now — because the sellers are not willing to lower the price to get a sale. They still want to make what their next-door neighbors made a few years ago, but that is not going to happen for a while. Several years ago, when the market was hot, you would have two or three offers on a home, and when buyers looked at a home, they wanted to put in an offer. It was not a matter of 'We will come back later; let's look at some more houses.' Now the market has slowed down and there is no sense of urgency for buyers, so they are willing to sit and wait and see if sellers will come down in price."

An investor also wants to avoid overpaying for improvements and repairs at his or her properties. Overpaying can occur when a property needs an emergency repair and the investor is caught unprepared, without the name of a reliable person to call. To avoid this problem, the investor, as part of his or her due diligence, should get in touch with several contractors or handymen in the area to compare their estimates of the cost of materials and labor. The investor should also develop a roster of repair persons whom he or she can call.

Buying Too Much Property

Seized by an initial surge of enthusiasm, a novice investor may buy "too much house;" that is, an investor with no prior landlord experience may buy a fourplex where many repairs are needed and the tenants are hostile and not easily appeased. This could quickly discourage the investor and make him or her question the wisdom of investing in multiunit residential properties.

A variation of this occurs when an investor buys a fixer-upper but lacks the time and skills to do the improvements and lacks the funds to hire contractors or a handyman to do the fixing up. As a result, the property may be off the resale or rental market for a long time, which defeats the purpose of the purchase in the first place.

A beginning investor in mobile homes or mobile-home parks can commit the same type of error. A novice investor may come across a 75-space mobile-home park that has been around for several decades and is in foreclosure. There may be issues about park management, about chronically late payments of lot rents by mobile home owners or tenants, about repairing old mobile homes or bringing in newer ones, and about the adequacy of the unit rentals.

Before jumping into this nest of difficulties, the investor should consider whether he or she has the time and ability to tackle all the problems that plague the mobile-home park. As many experienced investors point out, it is not enough to offer seller financing as a means to attract people to the park. The owner must make the park itself attractive, must install competent managers to run it efficiently, and must put in residents who are responsible and respectable.

Buying Far From Home

A smart investor does not want to own a building out of town. To ensure that his or her properties are in good condition and maintaining or even improving their value, an investor does not want to live so far away that he or she cannot exercise proper oversight. Even if the property is in the hands of a management company, the investor must keep an eye on the managers to make sure they are taking good care of the property and properly handling tenant issues.

Emotional Attachment

An investor must keep his or her mind on the investment plan and an eye on the bottom line when considering properties. If the investor has the proper "business is business" attitude, he or she realizes that there is no place for emotional attachment in the evaluation of an investment property. Instead, the investor must maintain a detached attitude and be prepared to walk away from a property if the numbers do not work out, even if the property has a picket fence and a house that reminds the investor of grandma's old place.

After buying a property, the investor must continue to be emotionally detached from the house. This means not over-improving the property to suit the investor's taste. It also means refraining from saying anything if the tenants' personal habits are different from those of the investor (provided the property is not being damaged). It could be that a tenant's clothing is strewn all over the living room, that dirty dishes are piled all over the kitchen, or that the tenant sleeps all day. The investor must remember that the unit is the home of the tenant, who pays rent in exchange for the right to enjoy his or her home.

Unrealistic Expectations

An investor in residential properties must be patient and realistic about the profits that he or she can expect to make. Some experts have said that a profit that exceeds 10 percent per year is a good return from rental properties, but they have also acknowledged that many investors with small portfolios earn less, even after appreciation is factored in. Moreover, a "good" return in one area may be considered low in another area. For example, a 7 percent return may be considered respectable in a city where properties are costly, while 8.5 percent may be the threshold of success in a lower-priced market.

It is also inadvisable to depend on tax breaks as a means of turning a profit on a property.

Over-Financing

An investor may get carried away and borrow too much money to purchase a property, which can happen when an investor gives the seller a second mortgage to secure part of the balance on the purchase price after making the down payment, while also taking out a first mortgage for more than the amount of the remaining balance that the seller is owed.

To see how this plays out, consider this scenario:

> $250,000 purchase price
> - 25,000 down payment
> $225,000 balance owed
> 150,000 amount of lender first mortgage
> +125,000 amount of seller second mortgage
> $275,000 total borrowed

An investor may not be able to get the cash flow from the purchased property to cover both mortgage loans. In the event of a foreclosure, the seller could lose a substantial portion, if not all, of the amount owed under the second mortgage because the first mortgage will enjoy priority for satisfaction of the underlying debt. Questions might also be raised about whether a fraud had taken place.

At any rate, this kind of financing arrangement is extremely perilous for the buyer and the seller because the buyer is effectively borrowing profits before they are generated.

Other Financing Pitfalls

Another financing problem for the unwary buyer can occur when the interest rate offered by a conventional lender is not locked in and the purchase and sale contract is not properly worded to protect the buyer. As attorney Estelle Flynn Lord explained:

"I like to find out from the buyers what their limit is. It did not matter so much a few years ago when the interest rates were extremely low, but with rates creeping up now, it is important that buyers have a limit. In other words, that if the interest sought by the lender at the time of the closing has risen above a specific rate, the buyers do not have to go through with the purchase."

Problems also may occur when, in their eagerness to own a property free and clear as soon as possible, buyers take out loans with short repayment terms. Whether a seller or a conventional lender is providing the financing, the longer the repayment term is, the lower the payment will be. Therefore, the better course for a buyer may be to stretch out the payment schedule as long as possible. Some experts recommend that terms be no less than ten years. A low mortgage payment will put less pressure on the property to produce sufficient cash flow to cover all the costs. This reasoning will not apply if the buyer is more interested in appreciation and has the resources to sustain minimal, or even negative, cash flow.

Skipping the Property Inspection

An investor will pour several thousands of dollars into the purchase of a residential property. He or she will pay a lender's various fees and the attorney's fees. Yet, the investor may be tempted to "save" $300 or $400 by not having a professional inspect the property. This is a "savings" that can cost much more in the future when one or more serious problems emerge. The problem could be an $8,000 roof replacement or a $4,000 furnace replacement — or worse.

The desire to keep a handle on expenses is understandable, particularly as the costs leading to the closing start to add up, but the property inspection is not the item to cut. A good property inspector will uncover serious structural or systemic defects and can alert the investor of conditions that could make obtaining insurance extremely difficult, such as when an older house has knob-and-tube electrical wiring, which will cause nearly all insurers to decline coverage.

Tenancy Errors

After buying a property and proceeding to rent it, the investor takes on the role of landlord. The relationship with tenants can be a minefield for the careless landlord. See Chapters 15 through 18 for further examination of the landlord/tenant relationship.

Failing to Screen Tenants

Although the people who will rent a unit will likely be strangers, the landlord can and should take steps to learn as much relevant information about them as possible before renting to them. Not only may this involve checking credit reports and employment status, it also means finding out from previous landlords what type of tenant a prospect was. The investor can find out whether the tenant ran loud parties late into the night. Screening can also reveal whether the tenant physically assaulted the landlord, family members, or others or allowed his or her children to draw on the walls.

Mike Hurney, an experienced real estate investor near Boston, told a cautionary tale about renting to tenants who are not properly screened. In his early days as a landlord, Hurney was renting an apartment in Salem, Massachusetts, to three people. Different people came and went, and eventually, only one man remained in the apartment. Hurney picks up the story:

"I had not bothered to check the credit of the person who was left living in the apartment. When he was late with the rent, I went over there, introduced myself, and asked about the rent. The guy said, 'I am gearing up my campaign. I can give you half the rent now and the other half after the election.' I said, 'What election? What are you talking about?' The guy told me his name and said he was running for mayor of Salem. Then I realized that he had posters all over town about his campaign. In the ensuing months, he got behind further and further in the rent. I did not dare start eviction proceedings because what if he did get elected? So I waited until he lost the election, and I went down to file the papers to evict him. In the middle of the court case, I get a letter from a woman who wrote, 'I noticed that you are evicting [*name omitted*]. If you had come to us, the National Tenant Network, for our credit-screening services, you would have noticed that he was kicked out of his last three apartments.' I called her right away and asked how she knew that.

She said her company has people who check the housing court records weekly."

The lesson to be learned is that, before allowing anyone to occupy a unit, the owner must have as much pertinent information as possible about the person. This measure can go a long way toward averting many future headaches.

Accepting Tenant Excuses

If a landlord has properly screened the tenants, he or she is less likely to experience the nonpayment or late payment of rent. In the event that such problems do arise, a landlord must not casually accept tenant excuses for failing to pay the rent on time. Landlords can be sympathetic with their own family and friends, but that type of sympathy has no place in a landlord/tenant relationship.

This does not mean refusing to work with a tenant who is going through a temporary rough patch. Nevertheless, landlords cannot afford to feel sorry for their tenants and must decide whether they are in business to make money or to be kind.

Inadequate Leases

After screening a tenant, the most important way that a landlord can protect his or her interests is with the lease. If a lease is worded poorly or contains terms not recognized by the landlord/tenant laws of the state, the landlord will have a difficult, even impossible, time evicting a troublesome tenant.

The landlord can have his or her attorney draft a lease. Alternatively, the landlord can contact the local landlord or apartment owners' association for up-to-date lease forms and related information.

The Anonymous Landlord

Experienced investors hold different opinions about whether they should reveal themselves as owners to their tenants. One view is that an owner should not hesitate to visit his or her properties and meet the people who are paying the rent, as investor Mike Hurney found out:

"When I first started, I thought that the tenants did not want to know who I was, so I would go over to the buildings and pretend I was the manager or the maintenance guy. I never looked them in the eye or anything. But I found they really want to know who owns the building. At any rate, nowadays, you can give a kid a couple of bucks and he can get on the Internet and find out who owns anything. I get a kick out of landlords who say, 'I have an unlisted number and a P.O. box.' You want to bet how long it will take me to find out what they own?"

John Hyre, who invests in mobile-home parks, had a contrary view.

"I never tell the renters that I am the owner. If they know you are the owner, they get a sense of 'You owe me. You have money.' One tenant told me, 'You have money so I'm not paying you the rent because you don't really need it and I do.' Obviously that conversation did not go well. But if the renters think that you are the manager — for example, you show up unshaven in a pair of jeans and a flannel shirt in a beat-up car and take an 'I'm just John the manager' approach — there is much less confrontation and attitude. I strongly recommend that approach."

In any case, barring problems, it should not be necessary for a landlord to keep returning to a property after it is rented. The landlord/tenant relationship is based on a business transaction. It is not a channel for making friends, socializing, or snooping.

Poor Maintenance

A property that is maintained poorly will perform poorly. It will cause good tenants to leave, it will not command market rents, it will not attract good replacement tenants, and, not surprisingly, it will not provide adequate cash flow or sell for a good price. Additionally, the longer that problems are ignored, the larger and costlier the problems will become. A prime example of this is water that seeps into a basement. If the opening that allows the seepage is not sealed, in time, more water will make its way into the basement.

A smart landlord will train the tenants to report problems, even if they seem small, as early as possible. The landlord can then decide whether the problems should be addressed right away.

You do not want to be the owner who deferred maintenance for years and must sell at a deep discount.

14

How and When to Sell

For every investor, the time comes when it is necessary or desirable to sell one or more assets. When those assets are residential properties, the motivation to sell could be that a property has become too troublesome or unprofitable to merit a place in the investor's portfolio. It also could be that the sale of a property will provide funds for the leveraged purchase of several other properties. Another possibility is that an investor wants to sell a few properties to invest in other types of assets or to acquire a reward, such as a vacation home or a boat.

Although market conditions and the shifting needs of an investor play their parts in the decision to sell, a properly formulated investment plan should be the primary source for guidance on when and how to sell a duplex, triplex, fourplex, mobile home, or mobile-home park. In other words, the investor must be able to articulate his or her investment goal before placing a property on the market, and the investment plan should specify how to "exit" from a property in a way that fulfills the goals of the investor. Without proper planning, an investor may end up selling, for less than its true value, a property that has been improved, maintained, and filled with good tenants or paying capital gains taxes that could have been deferred.

Reasons to Sell

There are many good reasons for an investor to sell a property. Some of these reasons are:

- Property bought as a fixer-upper is rehabbed and now ready for sale

- Neighborhood value and appearance are deteriorating

- Deterioration of a house makes repairs too expensive

- Owner has tired of being a landlord

- Divorce judgment requires a couple to sell its home or investment properties and split the profits

- Owners want the freedom and funds to travel

- Partnership that owned the property is dissolving or no longer exists

- One or more owners have died, and no heir wants the property

Most of the reasons on this list are self-explanatory, but two of them bear closer examination. When investors rather than homeowners are buying houses in a neighborhood, this may signal that the neighborhood and the prices of the homes in it are on a downward slide. Additionally, when an old house becomes too expensive and time consuming to upgrade and will return in value only a small percentage of the costs of improvements, it may be time to sell the house as a fixer-upper.

The following are bad reasons to sell a property:

- Disappearance of leverage on houses owned free and clear

- Loss of depreciation on houses owned a long time

- Unsolicited offers to buy an investor's property

Investors who have paid off the loans on properties may be quick to sell out of concern that there is no more leverage and that the rate of return will therefore be low. The problem with this line of reasoning is that it disregards (1) the significantly increased cash flow that is created when the mortgage debt is extinguished and (2) the leverage that continues to exist when an investor owns some properties free and clear and some properties that are encumbered by mortgage debt.

As for concerns about depreciation, a house that has been owned for so long that it offers no more depreciation remains a valuable asset if it provides good returns, is in a good area, and is in good shape. An investor who wants or needs depreciation can buy other properties that offer it.

Finally, buyers will always be attracted to well-kept, well-managed properties. Prudent investors should keep their best-performing properties and sell the weaker ones in their portfolios first.

Methods of Selling

After an investor has determined that there are valid reasons to sell one or more of his or her properties, the next decision is how to effectuate the sale.

Outright Sale

An investor may want to receive the proceeds of a sale without retaining any interest in a property. Assuming that the investor has carefully considered the relevant tax consequences, an outright sale will be the way to go. The investor will receive either all cash from the buyer or a combination of a cash down payment and a check from a mortgage lender that provides the financing to the buyer.

An all-cash deal can close quickly, if there are no complications. In contrast, a transaction that involves a mortgage from a conventional lender can take six weeks or more to close.

Lease/Option

Instead of an outright sale, a short-term lease with the option to purchase will be a better fit with some investment plans. The lease/option is an ideal way to sell a property for retail price. It is an arrangement that is attractive to individuals who want to buy property but do not immediately qualify for a conventional mortgage because of poor credit or inadequate income. The lease/option also can save the seller the commission that a real estate agent would earn.

The components of a lease/option arrangement are the sale price of the property, the option payment, and the monthly rental amount. The "optionee" pays the owner for an option (also referred to as a down payment) to buy the property at a later time. The optionee also makes monthly rental payments for the duration of the lease. The owner credits an agreed-on portion of the monthly rent toward the purchase price. If the optionee later wants to exercise the purchase option, he or she must qualify at that time for a conventional loan or must pay the balance of the purchase price with other funds.

There is significant interplay among the components of a lease/option arrangement. The owner may set the price of the property higher in exchange for a lower option payment and a lower monthly rent. If the owner sets the option payment at a higher level and the optionee does not buy the property, the owner keeps the option payment; the owner's profit remains the same, even if the optionee does buy the property. A higher monthly rent produces a higher cash flow for the owner, but the rent sought by the owner must not be so high that it discourages interest in potential renters and leaves the property vacant for too long. According to investors experienced in lease/option arrangements, of all the components, price has the greatest effect on profit.

Experienced investors also report that higher option payments are more likely to result in purchases by optionees than are lower option payments. This is because an optionee who has paid more up front for a property is more motivated to complete the purchase. At the same time, the credit market has an effect on how many lease/options end in sales. When interest rates rise and it becomes difficult to obtain conventional financing without high credit scores, fewer individuals qualify for loans, and they are unable to complete the sale. In contrast, when interest rates drop and financing becomes easier to find, more individuals qualify for conventional loans and are able to buy properties under a lease/option.

Before agreeing to a lease/option, the seller must find out why the prospective optionee does not qualify for a conventional loan. If it is a matter of a few late payments on a credit card or another credit or income problem that can be fixed in a short time, the seller could agree to a lease/option, as long as the other tenant-screening methods return positive results.

As with a regular tenancy, the owner will receive the option payment and rent for the first month. Nevertheless, the total up-front payment sought by the owner must not be so high that it discourages prospective buyers. Again, as with a regular rental, the location and condition of a property determine how much the owner can charge on a lease/option.

For the length that the lease term should be, shorter is better than longer. If property prices surge during the lease term, an owner bound by a lease/option to a specific sales price stands to lose a significant amount of profit.

For this reason, some experts recommend one-year lease terms; if the optionee needs more time to fix credit problems, the owner may extend the option period for one year for a higher purchase price and a higher monthly rental amount. If the owner knows from the beginning that the optionee's credit problems will require more than a year to fix, the lease term can be longer, such as two or three years.

There are many reasons why an optionee may not be able to complete the purchase of a property. Aside from the obvious one of not qualifying for a mortgage, an optionee may get married or divorced, become ill, or be transferred by an employer. Offering to return a portion of the option payment if the optionee has taken care of the house and has paid rent on time is an effective tactic. This treatment of the option payment as a security deposit provides optionees an incentive to move — thus saving on eviction costs — and to return the property in good condition. The investor would then free to make another lease/option arrangement with a different person.

Installment Sale

An investor's plan may call for the gradual sale of residential properties, coupled with the transfer of responsibility for upkeep and taxes. Under this scenario, the investor plays the roles of seller and of mortgage lender to a qualified purchaser.

This can be a win-win situation for the seller and the purchaser. The seller defers capital gains taxes while receiving monthly payments, free of the landlord responsibilities of maintenance, insurance, and real property taxes, and the purchaser gains title to a home through means other than a conventional mortgage.

There are other advantages when a seller takes back a mortgage. For the buyer, there is no need for an appraisal and its related expense. This allows the seller to price a property higher than the amount at which it might have appraised if a conventional lender had been involved. For some buyers who are determined to own a home, despite their limited means, the focus will be the affordability of the monthly payments, rather than the price of the property, which will be paid over time.

The interest rate charged and the length of the mortgage term determine the amount of the monthly payments, and these two factors give the seller considerable flexibility. Moreover, the IRS treats this type of transaction as an "installment sale," which allows the seller to stretch out over time the payment of the capital gains tax.

The seller might insist on a nonrefundable down payment, although the better practice is to have the purchaser make one in a show of good faith. The next decision is how much of a down payment to make. A down payment that is not too low has the psychological effect of motivating the buyer to keep his or her part of the bargain. Conversely, a buyer who has made a small down payment may not think twice about defaulting on the monthly mortgage payments and even moving out in the dead of night.

Of course, before drawing up a note and mortgage to formalize the installment sale, the seller will need a credit report on the buyer and will verify the buyer's ability to make the mortgage payments. It could be that the buyer looks forward to being a first-time homeowner, but his or her credit score is not sufficiently high to satisfy a conventional lender. Nevertheless, the buyer may never have missed or been late with a rental payment and may have enough income to cover the monthly mortgage payments. The seller may also ascertain that the property is not more than the buyer can reasonably handle in terms of the payments, the maintenance, and the responsibilities of a landlord to tenants in the other units in the building. If all these factors line up properly, the seller may judge that he or she should go through with the deal because the risk of having to take back the property from the buyer is minimal.

On the other hand, if the buyer lives far away from the property, has no plans to move onto the property, and has no definite plan for managing it, the seller could calculate that the risk of default would be too high.

In short, a seller who no longer wants a property and the landlord responsibilities that come with it will want to avoid the trouble and expense of foreclosing on a defaulting buyer and ending up with the property again. To do this, the seller must do his or her homework about the buyer.

Seller Wraparound Mortgage

Depending on the particular needs of a seller and a buyer, the wraparound mortgage may be a suitable variation of seller financing, though it is not often advised and is illegal in some states. In a wraparound mortgage, the seller does not pay off the one or more mortgages that exist on his or her property. Instead, the seller "wraps" a new loan around the existing loans. In other words, a new, larger loan is created, and the unpaid balances of the existing loans (also known as the underlying mortgages) become part of the wraparound mortgage. The buyer pays the seller on the wraparound mortgage, and the seller makes the monthly payments on the underlying loans and pockets what is left over. The wraparound mortgage is subordinate to the underlying mortgages, which means that the underlying mortgages will be paid first and the wraparound mortgage after them, in the event of a foreclosure on the property.

To see how a wraparound mortgage works, assume that Bonnie Buyer has agreed to purchase a duplex from you for $250,000. You had bought the property for $200,000. Your payments on a first mortgage with a balance of $60,000 are $400 per month, and your payments on a second mortgage with a balance of $40,000 are $300 per month. Your equity in the property would be $100,000 (the down payment and capital improvements you made are omitted for purposes of this example). Bonnie pays you a $25,000 down payment, and you take back a wraparound mortgage of $225,000. At an 8 percent interest rate over a 12-year term, the monthly mortgage payments from Bonnie would be about $2,436.

This is how much you would pay on the underlying mortgages, and how much you would pocket:

$2,436 mortgage payment per month from Bonnie Buyer
 - 700 payments per month on two underlying mortgages
$1,736 per month net to seller

Added to the monthly mortgage payments from the buyer will be an amount that the seller, much like a conventional lender, will escrow for the payment of the property taxes and insurance.

The wraparound mortgage arrangement can prove profitable to the seller when the interest rates on the underlying loans are notably lower than the rate on the wraparound mortgage.

Nonetheless, the "due on sale" clause in one or more of the underlying mortgages may pose a problem. That clause, which is present in most mortgages, states that the entire balance of the loan is due when title to the mortgaged property passes to another person. Sellers often try to circumvent this problem by entering into a "contract for deed" with the buyer. Under a contract for deed, an installment sale takes place, but the buyer does not receive title to the property until he or she has paid off the wraparound mortgage. Thus, not only is the seller paid in full before title passes, but the underlying mortgages are also paid in full.

Sellers who are contemplating contracts for deeds should seek the assistance of an attorney. This is because one or more of the underlying mortgage lenders may reject the reasoning behind the contract for deed and instead may take the position that an actual sale has transpired and that the seller must immediately pay the entire balance of the underlying loan.

The seller also must be aware that his or her insurance requirements as the buyer's lender vis-à-vis the insurance requirements of the underlying lenders could present issues that must be finessed. These issues will stem from the requirement that the lender be listed as an "added insured" on the policy that covers the property.

Tax Consequences

As noted in Chapter 2, the sale of an investment property triggers the capital gains tax.

As explained at **www.irs.gov**, the U.S. tax code classifies capital gains and losses as short-term or long-term, depending on how long the taxpayer holds a property before selling it. If the property was held for one year or less before it was sold, the capital gain or loss is short term, and if the property was held for more than one year before the sale, the capital gain or loss is long term. The tax rates that apply to net capital gain — which is the amount by which a taxpayer's net long-term capital gain exceeds his or her net short-term capital loss — may be lower than the tax rates that apply to other income. These are called the maximum capital gains rates. For the year 2007, the maximum capital gains rates were 5 percent, 15 percent, 25 percent, or 28 percent. The allowable annual deduction for capital losses that exceed capital gains is $3,000 (or $1,500 if a taxpayer is married and filing separately); the allowable amount of the capital loss that exceeds the capital gains is subtracted from other income reported on the taxpayer's tax return.

Note: The 5 percent capital gains tax was reduced to zero in 2008. Because the tax laws change frequently, it is important to consult a tax professional for the latest information.

The most common tax rate on a net capital gain is 15 percent. If the net capital loss exceeds this limit, the taxpayer can carry the loss forward to later years.

One legal way to delay the payment of capital gains tax is the 1031 exchange, which allows the investor to roll all the net proceeds from the sale of one property into the purchase of another property of "like kind." The 1031 exchange also can be useful to an investor who no longer wants to manage several small properties, such as duplexes. The investor can sell all the duplexes and then use the proceeds of the sales to buy one property, such as a fourplex.

The criteria for a 1031 exchange are complicated, but the key to using the exchange and avoiding a "taxable event" is timing. After the sale of a property is completed, the investor has 45 days to identify up to three new properties from which one will be selected as the "replacement" property. The closing must occur either within 180 days of the sale of the "relinquished" property or by the due date for the filing of the tax return for the year in which the relinquished property was sold. The investor is not permitted to handle the exchange and instead must use the services of an independent "qualified intermediary" (or "1031 exchange agent") who will hold in escrow all the proceeds from the sale of the relinquished property and will prepare the paperwork of the 1031 exchange.

The personal residence exemption under the U.S. tax code is another way to avoid the capital gains tax. The exemption applies to an owner who has been living in a one- to four-family house. An owner who is single pays no tax on the first $250,000 gain, and a married couple filing jointly pays no tax on the first $500,000 gain. To qualify for the personal residence exemption, a taxpayer must satisfy two tests.

- The ownership test: the taxpayer must have owned the house for at least two of the preceding five years

- The use test: the taxpayer must have lived in the house as his or her main residence for at least two years

If a couple is claiming the exemption, the requirements are as follows:

- Either spouse must pass the ownership test

- Both spouses must pass the use test

- Neither spouse must have claimed the personal residence exemption in the preceding two years

When a seller provides the buyer with financing and takes back a mortgage, the IRS considers the transaction an installment sale. The seller does not have to pay the capital gains tax all at once. Instead, the seller pays the tax only on the amount of the monthly payments from the buyer that is attributed to principal.

The tax information mentioned here is meant only to alert investors to some of the ways that the tax laws treat different sales transactions. Investors are strongly advised to seek the assistance of tax professionals for information and strategies that fit their particular circumstances and needs.

Prepare the Property for Sale

An investor can take inexpensive steps to prepare a property for sale. The goal is to make the property stand out from similar properties on the market that will be competing for attention. One of the most common ways to instantly upgrade a property is to paint the interior walls. A fresh coat of paint makes a unit look clean and well-kept. If the carpet is dull and dirty, a good steam cleaning should brighten it, but if the carpet is too stained or torn, the investor may consider replacing it with an inexpensive grade.

Just as a homeowner is advised to spruce up the home's curb appeal before putting the home up for sale, investors also need to gauge the curb appeal of the residential properties they want to sell. This could be a simple matter of clearing trash from the front of the property, touching up the trim with paint, washing the porch and steps, cutting hedges, or mowing the lawn in the front and back of the building. A sure way to make a bad first impression on potential buyers is by leaving overgrown weeds or discarded toilets, gutters, and other debris on the property.

If there are major defects at the property, such as a roof or furnace that needs replacing, the investor must decide whether it makes more economic sense to correct the defects or to offer a discount on the sales price to a buyer who requests it.

Marketing the Property

The investor who wants to sell a property must decide whether to use the services of a real estate agent or to rely on him or herself to market the property and find potential buyers.

The decision of the investor will depend on how much motivation, time, and experience the investor has.

Undertaking to sell his or her own property requires that the seller:

- Advertise the property in newspapers and on the Internet

- Field calls and e-mails from interested persons

- Determine that a potential buyer is financially qualified to make the purchase

- Show the property to qualified potential buyers

- Prepare the sales contract

If the seller is uncomfortable or incapable of taking all these steps, the better course will be to have a real estate agent handle the marketing and showing of the property. Even so, the seller should keep an eye on the efforts of the agent to make sure that everything possible is done to find a qualified buyer.

Part III

MANAGING TENANTS AND PROPERTIES

15

KNOW THE LAW

Before a property manager can successfully deal with tenants, a thorough knowledge of the applicable laws is essential, from the federal Fair Housing Act to local and state ordinances. Tenants will have much access to assistance if they feel discriminated against, or maybe your expensive eviction case is lost on a technicality. So your deep understanding of housing laws — and the services of an experienced attorney — will assist you in preventing problems and protecting your business interests. No defense ever succeeded with "I did not know."

Federal Fair Housing Act

The federal Fair Housing Act, which is part of the 1968 Civil Rights Act, mandates that landlords may not refuse to rent, sell, or negotiate housing with someone on the basis of race, color, national origin, religion, sex, familial status (including pregnant women), or handicap. Landlords may not falsely deny that housing is available or treat some tenants differently than others, such as in enforcement of lease violations (for example, late payment of rent) or such as charging a higher damage deposit to families with small children. Neither can advertising for the rental property state a preference for or against tenants of one group. Exceptions, such as for buildings noted as senior housing, may apply. For more detailed information, see the U.S. Department of Housing and Urban Development Web site, **www.hud.gov**. The Fair Housing Act text can be found here: **www.usdoj. gov/crt/housing/title8.php**.

Other federal laws that also apply to housing, especially if the housing takes part in any federal programs such as those administered by HUD, include the Americans with Disabilities Act and other related laws (more in Chapter 17) and the Age Discrimination Act of 1975. As to prospective tenants, when landlords use consumer reports, such as credit history, in their decision to deny a rental application, the Fair Credit Reporting Act requires specific disclosures to the applicant and protects his or her right to dispute the accuracy of the information in the credit history. For more information visit: **www.ftc.gov/os/statutes/fcrajump.shtm**.

Your State Laws

Individual states have fair housing laws for additional protected categories not listed in the federal law, such as political affiliation, change in marital status, military or veteran status, sexual orientation, being a victim of domestic abuse or having taken out a restraining order, source of income, and other criteria. Applicable state law is based on a property's location rather than where the owner resides.

But state housing laws cover more than just discriminatory rental practices. Property managers need to be aware of all state landlord/tenant laws, including lease restrictions, proper eviction procedures, repairs and maintenance requirements, and even the deadline for returning a tenant's security deposit after one moves out.

See your state's government Web site for information on housing laws and landlord/tenant rights and responsibilities. Other resources include: **www.**

fairhousinglaw.org (a portion of www.civilrights.org), which has links to state laws, and www.fairhousing.com.

Your Local Laws

Cities have their own laws on the books dealing with housing, from rent controls to building codes. City or local governments' housing departments may also have fair housing boards or councils to hear and investigate complaints and refer people to the state civil rights commission or other government or private agencies.

Local government housing departments may also have funding or tax breaks available for managers who rehabilitate foreclosures or maintain rental housing for low-income residents. City laws and programs should be available to the public at city government offices or Web sites.

As always, money is better and more economically spent on a qualified real estate attorney for advice rather than for a defense.

16

SELECTING YOUR TENANTS

When you buy a duplex, triplex, fourplex, or mobile home and then rent it out, you officially become a landlord with tenants. This is the part that makes many people hesitant, even nervous, about investing in residential properties. The word "landlord" may conjure up Dickensian images of snarling, money-hungry slumlords. Some investors encounter contempt, as longtime residential real estate investor Anna Mills of Toledo, Ohio, found in her early days as a landlady.

"I did this on my own for 17 years. I never ran into another investor. I never heard anything complimentary toward them, either. At most, I would hear talk about slumlords. Some people would ask, 'What do you want to do that for?' and others would ask why I didn't get a 'real' job."

The word "tenant" is equally loaded, perhaps bringing to mind angry, menacing ne'er-do-wells who gleefully pay no rent, trash their apartments, and refuse to move as the landlord repeatedly goes to court to try to oust them.

The landlord experience does not have to be that way. Just as you took many steps to minimize the risk of buying the wrong property, so too must you take steps to minimize the risk of renting to people who should not be your tenants.

To succeed as a landlord, you will need to do more than put individuals and families in your units and collect rents from them. You want to find tenants who will pay on time, take care of their living quarters, and give you as little trouble as possible.

As in any human endeavor, problems will arise, and you must be prepared to handle them. Richard Seltzer, an attorney and residential property investor in Jersey City, New Jersey, made the observation, "If you are doing business with tenants, you must have the personality to deal with them. They are human beings with problems, and the relationship of a landlord and tenant is a difficult one."

Mills added:

"Here is what I have to say about 'bad' tenants. When you hear all the horror stories, of course it is the one bad tenant a landlord will talk about. You ever hear about the 25 good tenants. It is all in how you train them. Tenants only know the parameters you give them."

When a piece of property is sold, the transaction ends; a new transaction begins when the new owner sells the property. In contrast, when a rental property is purchased and a tenant signs a lease, the landlord becomes part of a transaction that does not end until the lease does. If the landlord is lucky, the tenancy will pass without incident.

Sooner or later, something is bound to go wrong either at the property or with a tenant.

This chapter, and the ones that follow, will guide you on how to stop some tenant problems before they manifest and how to resolve others that crop up. As you read the suggestions in these chapters and apply them to real-life situations, you will develop expertise in sizing up prospective renters and dealing with the challenges presented by the tenants you select. The more experience you accumulate, the more comfortable you will be wearing the mantle of landlord.

Marketing Rental Property

There are several ways to let the public know that you have a unit to rent:

- Advertise in the classified section of local newspapers, church bulletins, or university publications

- List the property on **www.craigslist.com** or other Web sites

- List the rental with a real estate agent

- Place signs at your place of worship, local colleges, supermarkets, community centers, and place of employment

- Tell your family, friends, neighbors, and acquaintances

The methods you choose should not clash with the type of tenant you will consider. For instance, if you do not want to rent to students, do not place ads in college or university publications. If you would be uncomfortable renting to coworkers or their relatives, do not place a notice on the bulletin board at work or in the company newsletter. Make sure, however, that any ads comply with the Fair Housing Act and do not discriminate.

Showing the Property

Next you receive calls and e-mails from individuals interested in seeing the unit you advertised. Before agreeing to show the unit, ask the inquirers whether they are employed, where they work, how many people will be living with them, and how soon they would need to move in. Make a list of prospects who seem to meet your minimal qualifications — these will be the first ones to invite to the property.

If you own only a few rental properties, you will likely handle the showing of the property to prospective tenants rather than pay a real estate agent or a management company to do so. This can be a time consuming process.

Some experts suggest holding an open house to show a unit to several prospects on a specific day and within a specific amount of time. It is not advisable to advertise such an open house publicly, because you may end up with people who are merely curious and not qualified to rent from you. Instead, after you have spoken with several prospects who contacted you in response to your advertisements about the unit, you can invite the ones who seem qualified to the open house. This should lead to several applications from interested prospects.

If you prefer not to hold an open house, you will have to set individual appointments to show the property. Because of work schedules, many prospects will likely prefer to visit the property in the evening or on the weekend, and you must be prepared to accommodate this. If possible, schedule several showings on the same day. Before traveling to the property, call the prospects and verify their appointments.

Showing a unit at appointed times is essential when it is currently occupied by a tenant. You must give the tenant advance notice that you will be showing the unit, and you will have to arrange with the tenant how to gain access to the unit, whether the tenant will be present to let you in, which is the preferred way, or whether you will use a passkey. Try not to overwhelm the tenant with a stream of strangers going through the unit in one day. Also, understand that the tenant has no obligation to clean the unit and put it in order for a showing.

On the other hand, if the current tenant is leaving on bad terms, such as after an eviction, or if he or she does not keep the unit in a clean, orderly condition, it is preferable to wait until the tenant vacates the unit before showing it to prospective tenants.

If the unit is vacant, resist the urge to play "tour guide" as you show it to prospective tenants. You can let them into the unit and point out different rooms, but you must allow prospects to go through the unit at their own pace, within reason, and in the manner that they want to see it. This means that, while you may think that the features of the kitchen are the key "selling" point of the unit, a prospect may be more interested in the size of the master bedroom or in the amount of available storage space. Conversely, if the landlord sees that a prospect hesitates to go through the unit on his or her own, the landlord can take the lead in a matter-of-fact manner.

When a prospect expresses an interest in renting the unit, the first step is to discuss the terms of the rental. That includes the amount of the rent, the length of the lease term, the amount of the security deposit, and the due date of the monthly rent payments. Leases are examined in more detail in Chapter 17.

After a prospective tenant agrees to your terms, you must begin your background work.

Screening Prospective Tenants

Some would-be renters will try to impress you with their alleged job titles and backgrounds. Others will be barely intelligible. Still others will be straightforward, no-nonsense types.

You will be tempted to judge prospective renters by their appearance, speech, and attitude. You will be drawn to those who are well-dressed, well-spoken, and courteous, or even warm. Nonetheless, be aware of the applicable federal and state anti-discrimination laws, and resist the urge to decide on the spot to rent to a particular person. You must give all interested prospects the opportunity to apply in writing for the unit.

You will also hear many stories about why the prospects are looking for a place to live. Be professional, do not be swayed, and stick to your routine application process.

Preliminary Questionnaire/Lease Application

Many landlords develop questionnaires, or lease applications, that they present to prospective tenants as the first step in the screening process.

The questionnaire will ask for the name of the applicant and his or her spouse, the dates of birth and Social Security Numbers of both spouses, the number of people who will occupy the unit, and the names of the occupants. Other information requested includes:

- Current address, phone numbers, and e-mail address of the applicant

- Emergency contact name and phone number

- Quantity and types of pets owned

- Three previous addresses and phone numbers, names, and contact information of the landlords or management companies

- Two or three bank references, including branch addresses, phone numbers, contact persons, and amount of time the applicant has been a client there

- Information about current and previous employers: names of employers, positions held, how long held, address and phone number of employers, and contact persons

- Three references: names, phone numbers, and relation to applicant

- Convictions for crimes and periods of incarceration

Anna Mills not only invests in properties, but also manages fourplexes. She prefers to ask the questions on the application and to fill in the answers with prospective tenants because of what they can unexpectedly reveal about themselves.

"The things people tell you are just phenomenal. It is as if they forget you are a landlord because they are trying to get into your place. They will say things like, 'You can call my landlord, but he is not going to tell you anything nice because I am suing him — I sued my last 10 landlords.' And I am left to wonder who they think they are talking to."

The questionnaire should state that any misrepresentations on the form may lead to the denial of the application and that the signer acknowledges the information being given is true and correct to the best of his or her knowledge. The prospective tenant and his or her spouse, if any, must sign the application. Current privacy laws require that the signature page be separate from the rest of the application.

In reviewing the entries made by a prospect on the questionnaire, notice whether he or she has lived for short periods of time at different addresses and whether the work history indicates stability or frequent movement from job to job. You should also be aware that applicants sometimes have friends or relatives pose as employers or landlords and managers. To prevent this, try to independently verify the names and contact information of employers, landlords, and managers by looking in the phone book or on the Internet. You might also want to drive to the address given for the landlord or manager and try to speak with him or her personally.

Records Release Authorization

Some states may require a separate authorization signed by a prospective tenant for the release of credit, banking, employment, police, and other background records. Even if not required, it is a good idea to have a prospect sign such a form in the event of a legal challenge in the future.

Credit Reports

With the release authorization in hand, you need to decide whether a credit check is necessary. It used to be a simple matter of ordering credit histories for a small fee, but changes in privacy laws have imposed many mandates that landlords may not be able to meet. These mandates, which vary from state to state, may call for the person or entity requesting a credit report to have, among other things, an office with a door that locks, a sign, locks on file cabinets, paper shredders, and locks on the computers. Landlords must check the particular requirements of their states and also comply with the federal Fair Credit Reporting Act.

Nevertheless, a credit report will include information that is both overinclusive and imprecise in giving a landlord an accurate picture of a prospective tenant, as investor Anna Mills pointed out:

"Think of it this way: do you really need a credit score? Do you really care if applicants have medical, credit-card, or some other kinds of problems if they always paid their rent on time? You must focus. You can pull documents such as eviction reports or find out what the previous landlord says. Also, of course, you must verify employment."

On the other hand, a credit report can serve as the proverbial canary in the coal mine, as prospective tenants who do not pay their bills on time may not pay their rent on time either. A credit report can let you know if prospective tenants have been improving lately with the timeliness of their bill payments or if their problems are chronic. It can be valuable in evaluating potential tenants objectively and on an equal basis with others. There also are services available for landlords that not only supply credit reports, but also provide a background check package including liens, judgements, bankruptcies, rental history, criminial records searches, and employment verification.

If a prospect balks at completing the questionnaire and the information release permission form, tell him or her that doing so is a nonnegotiable precondition to signing the lease. If the prospect still refuses, then you are free to decline his or her application and consider another prospect.

Section 8 Tenancies

The U.S. Department of Housing and Urban Development provides housing subsidies to tenants based on the amount of rent they can pay for housing in the private market. Known as the Section 8 housing voucher program, or Section 8 for short, the program is administered by state and local government housing agencies and is targeted at individuals with incomes of below 30 percent to no more than 80 percent of the area median income. Since its creation in 1974, Section 8 has become the main source of federal housing assistance for low-income families, the elderly, and the disabled.

A family with a Section 8 voucher commonly pays 30 percent of its income for rent and utilities, with the voucher paying for the rest of those costs up to a limit, or "payment standard," set by the area housing agency. A housing agency may set the payment standard between 90 and 110 percent of the fair market rent, which is the amount that HUD estimates as the amount needed for rent and utilities in moderately priced housing units in an area.

HUD sets the fair market rents each year in metropolitan areas and non-metropolitan counties for units with different numbers of bedrooms. In most areas, HUD sets the fair market rent at an amount that is enough to pay rent and utilities at 40 percent of recently rented units in the area, not including new units. There are 28 metropolitan areas for which HUD has determined that 40 percent is insufficient to allow voucher holders to rent housing outside a few low cost neighborhoods; for those 28 areas, HUD calculates the fair market rent on the basis of 50 percent of the recently rented units.

The demand for Section 8 vouchers often exceeds the resources that are available to HUD and local housing agencies. This commonly results in long waiting periods, and local housing agencies may close their waiting lists when they have more families on the list than can be helped in the near future. When a family or an elderly or disabled person is given a Section 8 voucher, the recipient must locate housing within 60 days. Not every recipient is able to use the voucher within that time limit due to a shortage of moderately priced housing and the refusal of some landlords to participate in the Section 8 program; in such a case, the recipient loses the voucher, which is then awarded to someone else.

When a recipient of a Section 8 voucher finds a single-family house or an apartment to rent and reaches an agreement with the landlord about the terms of the lease, the local housing agency inspects the property and determines whether the proposed rent is "reasonable," meaning consistent with market rents for similar units in the area. After the housing agency approves the unit, the voucher recipient and the landlord sign the lease and the landlord and the housing agency sign a housing assistance payments contract that runs for the same period as the lease.

Here is how the Section 8 voucher program works. If the Section 8 administrator determines that the income of a tenant allows him or her to pay only $480 per month in rent, and $1,200 is the market rent for a three-bedroom house — such as one semi-detached unit of a duplex — the landlord would receive rent as follows:

$ 720 from Section 8
+ 480 from the tenant

$1,200 total per month

In the above example, the Section 8 subsidy is 60 percent of the monthly rent, and the portion paid by the tenant is 40 percent. The subsidy can be an even higher percentage when a tenant is on a fixed income, such as disability payments. It can also be reduced if the tenant begins receiving income from a second source, such as a working spouse.

At any rate, a landlord can be confident that a Section 8 subsidy check will arrive in the mailbox each month, because the federal government guarantees the payment. In addition, the fear of losing the Section 8 subsidy for failure to meet their end of the bargain will motivate most Section 8 tenants to pay their portion of the rent in full and on time. If this turns out not to be the case and a tenant is constantly delinquent with payments without justifiable reason, the landlord should report the problem to the Section 8 administrator, who will deal with the tenant directly.

By the same token, the landlord takes on certain responsibilities when it rents to Section 8 tenants. These include keeping the unit up to the HUD Code, providing the services it agreed to in the lease, and notifying the local housing agency within a specific time of any intention to raise the rent. The local housing agency may send an inspector each year to verify that the property is up to the HUD Code. The housing agency can stop paying the monthly subsidies if an inspector finds that the building is not up to code and the landlord fails to take corrective measures.

Although these yearly inspections may seem annoying, they are precisely why some insurers of rental properties look favorably on rentals to Section 8 tenants. The insurers figure that the inspections prevent landlords from ignoring their maintenance responsibilities, which would lead to degrading the value of the property.

Section 8 also provides housing assistance vouchers for manufactured-home space rental, which the program considers a "special housing type." This assistance is for owners of manufactured homes who need to lease space for the home. The rent that is listed as payable to the owner of the space includes the owner's maintenance and management fees and the utilities that the owner pays. The local housing agency determines whether the rent to the space owner is reasonable when compared with the rent paid for other comparable "unassisted" spaces.

Recipients of Section 8 housing vouchers may represent an untapped market of renters for a landlord with multifamily units to fill. Some landlords have had negative experiences with Section 8 tenants, such as trashed apartments. Nevertheless, it is the landlord who chooses the tenant; the Section 8 program does not dictate where a voucher recipient will live and cannot force a landlord to accept a voucher recipient.

For more information about the Section 8 housing voucher program, see **www.hud.gov**.

Beware of the Professional Tenant

The professional tenant is someone who is intimate with the protections of various laws, can talk his or her way into a rental, and can manipulate situations for self-serving purposes.

Residential real estate investor Mike Hurney from Massachusetts has had several brushes with the professional tenant. He tells the story of a woman who wanted to rent a four-bedroom apartment from him. While Hurney was at the apartment making some repairs, the woman went to his home with her children and spoke with Hurney's wife about the rental. The woman then went over to the apartment.

"The woman showed up and said, 'I spoke with your wife, and she said it was OK. Where are the keys?' I said, 'Wait a minute. Do you have a deposit?' She said she gave the deposit to my wife. When I said that I wanted to go see my wife first, the woman said, 'Wait a minute. Here is the check.'"

Hurney noticed that the check was certified and made payable to "Michael Hurley." He found this odd because his wife always handed prospective tenants business cards with Hurney's name on them. He called his wife and learned that she had not obtained the usual background report on the woman. By the time Hurney arrived home, the service that he used had issued a preliminary report.

"It turned out that the woman was the chief of staff of a Massachusetts legislator. The background report said she had been evicted from one house and owed $27,000, and from another house, for which she owed $7,000 in rent. When I called the legislator for a reference, he said he depended completely on the woman and that she was the greatest person he had ever known. This flew in the face of the background report. Then I realized what the deal was with the check. I probably could have deposited it, but because it did not say my name exactly, the woman could have accused me of fraud and obtained the return of the money."

When he drove out to return the check to the woman at the address that she had given him, Hurney learned inadvertently that she was being evicted from there for $4,000 in back rent. Moreover, the "little puppy" that the woman had claimed to own was actually a St. Bernard.

17

THE LEASE AS YOUR ESSENTIAL TOOL

I n many localities, there are so-called month-to-month tenants. This means that there is no signed agreement, or lease, between the tenant and the landlord that sets out their understanding of the terms of the rental. Instead, their understanding is verbal. Either the landlord or the tenant can end the tenancy with sufficient notice, as defined by state law, and the tenant must move within a specific amount of time after receiving or giving the notice.

In contrast, a lease sets out the expectations of both the landlord and the tenant. For this reason, the lease is the most effective weapon a landlord has for dealing with a problem tenant who may have to be evicted. The lease can also provide the landlord with the best protection in case of a dispute with the tenant. Nevertheless, to be an effective tool for the landlord, the lease must be well crafted.

The quality of the lease document is significant because the law does not view landlords and tenants as being on equal footing; in the eyes of the law, the landlord enjoys a superior bargaining position. This means that the landlord is presumed to be more experienced and better equipped to dictate the terms under which a tenant will rent a unit. Under principles of contract law, because it is the landlord who provides the lease, the courts must interpret any ambiguities in the document against the landlord and in favor of the tenant. This is why it is crucial that the language in a lease be as clear and straightforward as possible and that it is not full of legal terminology that the average tenant will not be able to understand.

To ensure that a lease covers all the essential points, a landlord may want to have his or her attorney draft the first lease. If the tenancy is renewed under the same terms, other than the rent amount and the beginning and end dates of the lease, or if other units will be rented under the same conditions, the landlord can use the first lease as a model for the others. An alternative to an attorney-drafted lease may be a lease form available from the local landlord or apartment owners' association, although the form may be too generic to cover the particular circumstances of a tenancy.

Self-Explanatory Terms in a Lease

There are many terms that a lease must include. The essential, self-explanatory ones are:

- Names of the tenant and the landlord

- Address of the landlord

- Date the agreement is signed

- Address of the property being rented

- Dates that the rental begins and ends

- Amount of the rent — monthly (required) and annually (optional)

- Address to which the monthly rent must be sent; alternatively, instructions for the electronic deposit of the rent into a landlord bank account

- Rent due date — often the first of the month

- Name of the landlord or management company to which the monthly rental checks are to be made payable

- Penalty for late rent payments — typically applicable if rent is paid five days or more after the due date; a landlord may choose not to impose the penalty for the occasional late payment, but the lease should nevertheless provide for the penalty

- Fees for bounced (dishonored) rent checks; also applies to electronic transfers if there are insufficient funds in the tenant's account

- Requirement of certified checks or money orders for the rent payments

- Use of property — specifies that the unit is to be used only for residential purposes

- Occupants — specifies who will live in the unit, such as the tenant's children

- Guests — the tenant must notify the landlord in writing if someone will be a guest for more than a specific amount of time, such as two weeks

- Tenant must pay the rent for the first month up front

Other Terms in a Lease

A well-drafted lease also should address the following topics.

Security Deposits

A security deposit is money paid in advance by the tenant to the landlord as a guarantee against damages that may occur to the rented unit during the occupancy. Depending on applicable state law, a landlord may demand one and one-half months of rent as the security deposit. The law also may dictate where the landlord must hold the security deposit, often in a separate savings account that is listed as being "for the benefit of" the tenant. If there is no damage to the unit, the landlord must return the security deposit, with interest earned, when the lease ends and the tenant vacates the unit. The law may specifies how many days the landlord has after the lease ends to inspect the unit for damage and to notify the tenant if damage is found if the landlord intends to withhold the amount of the damage from the security deposit.

Normal Wear and Tear

Normal wear and tear is connected with the provision for security deposits because it states that "normal wear and tear" will not trigger the landlord's withholding of the security deposit. Normal wear and tear commonly refers to the use that a reasonable person made of the wood floors, carpets, kitchen counters, and other items in a unit during the tenancy for the purposes for which the items were intended. "Normal wear and tear" can be interpreted in highly subjective ways and may lead to litigation by tenants who believe that a landlord has improperly withheld their security deposits.

Sublet/Assignment

In this clause, the tenant is prohibited from subletting the unit or assigning his or her interest in the leased unit without the written consent of the landlord. This prevents the tenant who signed the lease from making a profit on the rental amount and from having unscreened individuals occupying the unit.

Condition of the Property

This clause states that the tenant has inspected the unit and agrees that it is in "habitable condition," that all the appliances and fixtures are functioning, and that the property is ready to be occupied.

Repairs to the Property

There are a number of ways in which a repairs provision can be worded. Depending on what the state laws require, the provision may provide that the landlord is responsible for the repair of the major systems and components of the building, such as the heater, roof, and plumbing, and that the tenant is responsible for other specified repairs. Alternatively, the lease may state that the landlord is responsible for repairs that exceed a specific amount and that the tenant is responsible for repairs up to that amount.

Utilities

The best-case scenario is one in which the tenant pays for all the utilities for his or her unit. Some properties may have common areas between two or more units, such as hallways and stairs, and the landlord is responsible for the electricity to light those areas. A house also may be set up in a way that makes the landlord responsible for the sewer and/or water bills. The utilities provision explains who is responsible for which utilities.

Improvements and Alterations

Under this clause, the tenant may not perform improvements or alterations to the property without the written consent of the landlord. At the end of the tenancy, if the tenant has performed improvements or alterations, he or she must restore the property to its original condition.

Children

Federal and state fair housing laws have closed off the possibility of not allowing children to live in a rental unit, except in HUD-approved senior housing. Even if the property does not have a safe place for children to play, it is for the parent(s), not the landlord, to decide whether a child should live there. Neither may a landlord discriminate against families with children by charging a higher rent, demanding a larger security deposit, renting for shorter lease periods, or including fewer amenities in a unit. Moreover, a landlord cannot restrict any of its tenants from having access to the facilities on the property, such as a laundry room or recreation room, if there are no clear safety concerns.

Instead of cringing at the thought of having noisy, mischievous children in the rental units, a landlord should consider renting to families or individuals with children as good business. People who have children normally want to raise them in safe, decent neighborhoods and buildings, and after they have settled in and placed their children in school, they are less likely to want to move. Long-term renters are good for the cash flow of a property.

Tenants with Disabilities

Regulations under the federal Fair Housing Act require owners with properties of four or more units that were "built for first occupancy after March 13, 1991" to make reasonable accommodations, at their own expense, so that tenants with disabilities can enjoy the rental property on an equal basis with nondisabled tenants. Property owners also must make reasonable adjustments to their rules, procedures, or services when requested by a disabled tenant. For example, if practical, an owner must grant the request of a disabled tenant for a wider and more conveniently located parking space.

The Fair Housing Act regulations also recognize the right of disabled tenants to modify their living space at their own expense if:

- The modifications extend only to what is necessary to make the living space safe and comfortable

- The modifications do not make the unit unacceptable to the next tenant; if they do, the disabled tenant must agree to return the unit to its original condition before vacating it

- The tenant obtains the prior approval of the landlord and ensures that the work will be performed in a professional manner, with all the required government approvals and permits

- The tenant pays the funds necessary for the needed restoration into an interest-bearing escrow account to ensure that the work is completed and that there will be no liens against the property

Another federal statute, the Americans with Disabilities Act (ADA), prohibits discrimination against people with disabilities and requires that they have access to public areas. The ADA applies mostly to commercial and retail properties, not to private residential properties that were constructed before 1991. For the requirements that apply to newer properties, see **www. usdoj.gov/crt/ada.html**.

Regardless of any restrictions against pets, disabled tenants must be allowed to have in their units animals that assist them with their daily life activities. Additionally, the ADA mandates that disabled tenants be allowed to have pets as a "necessary and reasonable accommodation." Moreover, if a tenant who claims a condition such as depression asks to have an animal for emotional support or companionship, federal law requires landlords to consider the request and grant it if it is reasonable. Several states and municipalities provide additional legal protections to tenants who need "emotional support" animals.

Pets

The landlord must weight the pros and cons of allowing nondisabled tenants to have pets and then must specify what the policy is. If you decide to allow pets, the lease should state that only domestic pets can be kept and should specify the kinds of domestic pets that are allowed. Domestic pets are commonly understood to be dogs, cats, tropical fish, and nonpredatory birds. You also may demand a separate pet deposit to cover damage caused by dogs or cats. The amount of the pet deposit can range from $50 to rent for one month; you will need to check what the normal practice is in the area where the property is located.

If the rented unit is in an urban or suburban area and has a back yard, it may be unreasonable to prohibit the ownership of a dog, and you would be reducing the pool of prospective tenants. Nonetheless, you want to be careful to restrict the number of dogs and other pets that a tenant can keep on the property. Also consider restricting the type of dog that is permitted to the extent possible in your jurisdiction; for example, you may be able to prohibit more aggressive breeds because of liability issues that could arise if the animal attacks someone.

If the rental property is in a rural setting and has plenty of land, you can be more flexible about the type and quantity of pets that a tenant may keep.

Default by Tenant

It is illegal in most, if not all, of the United States for landlords to padlock a unit and take or throw out the property of a tenant who has defaulted in the rent payments or has breached the lease in some other way. The default clause in a lease states that the defaulting tenant has a specific amount of time — often three days — to "cure" the default. Landlords must be careful to follow the statutory requirements for the giving of a notice of default; the failure to do so can obliterate any attempts to evict the tenant. The lease continues uninterrupted if the tenant cures the default.

Default by Landlord

The lease should specify that if the landlord fails to abide by the terms of the lease, such as by not making necessary repairs, the tenant must notify the landlord of the breach in writing, preferably by certified mail or similar means. The landlord should be given a reasonable amount of time to cure the default.

Right to Quiet Enjoyment

The right to quiet enjoyment provision states the legally recognized principle that those who legally reside on a property are entitled to occupy and enjoy the premises without interference by others, including the landlord.

Inspections

A landlord has the right to periodically inspect its property to ascertain that the terms of a tenancy are being fulfilled. Moreover, the municipality, the landlord's insurer, and the Section 8 program (if applicable) may want to conduct their own inspections from time to time.

The inspection provision in a lease takes into account the tenant's right to quiet enjoyment by stating that such inspections may be conducted with notice to the tenant, often 24 hours in advance.

Megan's Law

Named after a New Jersey child who was sexually assaulted and murdered by a neighbor who was a convicted sex offender, Megan's Law is a federal statute that requires law enforcement agencies to keep a registry of convicted sex offenders. The statute also requires the agencies to disclose the addresses of certain sex offenders under specific circumstances. If a landlord fails to disclose to its tenants that a convicted sex offender lives in the community, the landlord may be liable for that failure if a child of a tenant is injured or killed by the offender. In addition, a landlord who rents to a convicted sex offender may be liable to families in the community whose children are injured or killed by the offender.

The Megan's Law clause in a lease explains the purpose of the law and can direct a tenant who has children to a specific law enforcement agency or

Web site where he or she can find out whether any convicted sex offenders live in the community. This effectively shifts to the tenant the responsibility for obtaining the information about the presence of convicted sex offenders in the area.

Environmental Disclosures

Many state laws and local ordinances require landlords to disclose in their leases whether lead, asbestos, radon, or mold are present on the property. These may have to be addressed in separate clauses.

Jurisdiction/Venue

This clause specifies that the laws of the state in which the property is located govern the terms of the lease and that any legal action that relates to the tenancy will be brought in the county where the property is located. The clause also can provide that the losing party will be responsible for paying the attorney fees and court costs incurred in a lawsuit incurred by the prevailing party.

Surrender of the Property

The surrender provision requires the tenant to give the landlord written notice — often 30 days before the end of the lease term — of the intention not to renew the lease. The provision also states that the tenant must return the keys to the landlord or the landlord's agent and that the property must be in the same condition it was in when the tenant began occupying it, excluding normal wear and tear.

Holdover Tenant

If a tenant refuses to surrender the property at the end of the lease, he or she is considered a "holdover." When this happens, the landlord may choose to treat the tenant as a month-to-month tenant without a written lease but with the understanding that the terms of the lease apply as long as the tenant continues to pay rent on time. Alternatively, if the landlord wants the tenant out of the unit, the landlord will have to abide by the statutory notice requirements and either begin eviction proceedings or have the police remove the tenant as a trespasser, depending on what the law allows.

Abandonment

An abandonment clause commonly provides that, if a tenant leaves the unit before the end of the lease term and ceases to pay rent, the landlord has the right to enter the premises and take possession or dispose of any personal items left behind by the tenant. Landlords must determine whether state law prohibits this action.

Advertising by Landlord or its Agent

This provision states that, before the end of the lease — often 90 days prior — the landlord or the landlord's agent may advertise the unit for rent and may place signs on the property in an effort to find a new tenant. The provision also states that the current tenant must allow access to the unit so that the landlord or the agent can show it to prospective tenants. Specific dates and hours of availability for this purpose may be stated in the lease, as may the amount of notice that the tenant must receive in advance of a showing.

Sale of the Property

Similar to the advertising clause, the sale provision obligates the tenant to grant access to the unit, with notice, to allow the landlord or the landlord's agent to show the unit in connection with the sale of the property. The provision may state either that a sale would not affect the tenancy or that a new owner who seeks to occupy the unit will have the right to ask the tenant to leave at the end of the lease. Landlords must check the local laws on the rights of existing tenants in the event of a sale.

Rules and Policies

The lease may include the rules and policies that the landlord wants the tenants to follow. For example, various rules may state that any use of illegal narcotics on the premises by a tenant or guest of the tenant is grounds for eviction, that the tenant must notify the landlord in writing of any absences from the property that exceed two weeks, and that the tenant may not play music or instruments or make other loud noises on the premises after a specific time of night.

Common Areas

If a property has common areas, such as outside steps, a porch, or a corridor, a landlord should require the tenants to keep those areas free of clutter and easily accessible at all times. In other words, the common areas should be free of bicycles, baby carriages, boxes, or other items that would create a safety hazard in a fire or other emergency. This will be required by the insurer of the property as well as the local fire code.

Parking

In urban areas, tenants will appreciate having off-street parking. To avoid conflicts, a landlord should set a rule or specify in the lease that visitors are not allowed to park in the spaces reserved for other tenants. The landlord also should establish a policy on whether tenants are permitted to keep more than one vehicle, boats, or even campers on the premises.

In some areas, there is often little off-street parking, and the parking on the street is so tight that some cities go so far as to issue parking decals for residents and erect signs that prohibit nonresidents from parking on certain residential streets during specific hours. A landlord that is competing with other landlords for tenants may want to include a paid parking permit as a perk to a qualified applicant who signs a lease for a rental unit.

Local governments are responsible for enforcing handicapped parking requirements for multiunit rental properties. A landlord can find out the requirements at the local building and code enforcement office.

Recreational Facilities

Properties that are two- to four-family units are not likely to have recreational facilities such as pools and game rooms on site, but such facilities are common in large mobile-home parks.

No restrictions based on age may be imposed unless safety is a clear issue, such as children under a certain age unaccompanied by an adult in a pool area. Another consideration is that the ADA requires that disabled individuals have access to recreational facilities. Thus, if there are physical barriers in a pool area that prevent accessibility by the disabled, the property owner must remove the barriers at its own expense.

The landlord should establish a policy on how many people at a time can use a recreational facility, the hours that the facility can be used, and the condition in which the facility must be left after use (such as no taking of towels or chairs).

Joint liability clause

Whoever is of legal age and will be living in a unit should be listed as a party to the lease and should sign it. Whether a married couple, an unmarried couple, or two or more unrelated roommates will be occupying a unit, the landlord must protect him or herself. Married couples can separate and divorce, unmarried couples can go their separate ways, and roommates can come and go; for these reasons, a landlord should not risk a scenario in which no one in a unit wants to take responsibility for its care or for the rent payments. To prevent this, the lease should include a "joint and several liability" clause that makes the adult occupiers of a unit responsible, as a group and individually, for the entire amount of the rent.

If a tenant approaches you, the landlord, about allowing someone to take the place of a roommate who has moved out, you will need to do a background check on the new person. If he or she meets your criteria and the current lease term has not ended, you will want to substitute the new person for the one who moved away, by way of an addendum to the lease.

A word of caution on renting to unmarried roommates: some local jurisdictions prohibit landlords from renting to three or more unrelated individuals.

Final Words

The descriptions here briefly highlight the typical clauses found in residential leases. The specific wording of the terms of a lease will depend in large part on what the law requires and allows in the state where a property is located. Moreover, landlords are free to include other clauses, such as for "Miscellaneous Disclosures," as permitted by law and advised by their attorneys.

18

MANAGE YOUR TENANTS

Successful investors in residential properties have figured out that it is key to know how to manage the people who live on those properties. They understand that being a landlord is a business, not a hobby, and that it requires a certain mind-set for dealing with tenants, who are the clients of the business.

Many first-time investors have no experience as landlords. This should not be an obstacle. Like the other facets of becoming a successful investor, it is possible to learn the ins and outs of the landlord business. When applied to tenants, this means being familiar with the applicable laws and possessing or developing good "people skills."

Money, Property, and Tenants

Tenants will be paying the mortgage on the property on which they live, the real estate taxes, insurance, upkeep, and leftover cash that you pocket. In short, tenants are the engine of the cash machines that are residential properties.

Yet, as investor/property manager Anna Mills likes to remind new landlords, "Your money is not in the tenant. Your money is in the property." This means that landlords must view tenant problems as being temporary, not as insolvable and overwhelming. In the eyes of the law, landlords are the owners of their properties, and tenants have only a leasehold interest in it. Therefore, no matter how hard a troublesome tenant resists eviction efforts, eventually, the well-prepared landlord will win and get back the property.

One nightmare scenario cited by many would-be investors in residential properties centers on tenants who wreck their apartments before moving out, thus requiring the landlord to spend time and money to repair the damage before the apartment can be rented to someone else. Even if this was as common an occurrence as many believe, a landlord should not be perturbed by it and must learn to take it in stride as part of the business. As Mills observed, "There is no difference between buying a fixer-upper and getting back a property that has been trashed by a tenant. In both cases, you have the ability to go in there, update the place a little bit, and rent it out for more."

If a tenant has left behind stained carpets, streaked walls, and baked-on grease in the oven, the landlord needs to steam-clean or replace the carpets, paint the walls, clean the oven, and quickly put that money-making unit back on the rental market.

Existing Tenants

Landlords may find that their tenants want to know who owns the building. Landlords may have met some tenants briefly in the course of walking through their units before buying the property. After completing the purchase, a landlord should, and often must by law, send a letter to each tenant advising that he or she is the new owner, providing information on how to contact the landlord or property manager, and stating where to send the monthly rental payments. The letter may also state where the security deposits are being held and how requests for repairs should be made. The letter may also include the contact and employment information that the landlord has for the tenant and ask whether the information is correct or requires updating.

On the other hand, letting tenants know that there is a new owner may prompt some of them to test the new person's resolve by not paying their rent, paying it late, or making frequent, unreasonable demands for repairs and upgrades to their units. Perhaps a tenant was already like that and had run roughshod over the previous owner. In either case, the new landlord must act swiftly and decisively to show that he or she is in full command of the property and will not tolerate nonsense and leases being breached by the tenants.

Problem Solving

Learning to anticipate problems and handle the ones that spring up before they can grow out of proportion will go a long way toward preventing conflicts with tenants and giving peace of mind to a landlord.

Because being a landlord is a business, it is essential to keep good records. This involves maintaining a file on each unit in a building and on all the tenants who rent them. This will make it easy to quickly look up the history of a unit or a tenant.

Rent Collection

Collecting the rent is the number one responsibility of a landlord as a good investor. This is often not a problem, because most tenants pay their rent on time.

Those who fail to pay or who pay only partial rent must not be allowed to turn rent collection into a monthly game of catch-me-if-you-can. To prevent this, a landlord must have a system in place that is always triggered at the first sign of trouble, often when the penalty for late payment begins to run. The system involves warning the delinquent tenant in writing (but not e-mail, which may not hold up in court) of his or her failure to pay the rent as required by the lease, the amount of the rent due, and the number of days that the tenant has to make the payment. If the tenant does not pay the rent within the specified time, it is a good idea to send a second notice marked as such to the tenant. If the tenant still does not pay, it is time to file an eviction action in court for nonpayment of rent.

Landlords must be sure to comply with their state law requirements about the content of notices that are sent to tenants and the time for sending them. It is essential to create a paper trail of these notices, because this will form the basis of a case against the tenant if the matter goes to court.

Using written notices also cuts down on the need for personal visits to the property for face-to-face encounters with tenants. A personal encounter is likely to be a waste of time, because the landlord may have to listen to excuses as to why the tenant failed to pay the rent or follow the rules that are set forth in the lease.

The point is that the landlord must be in full, detached, business mode when dealing with tenants. As investor Anna Mills put it:

"While tenants are telling you that Aunt Susie just died for the third time and they had to travel to the funeral, you are very sympathetic, but at the same time, you are handing them the three-day eviction notice."

By enforcing the lease terms and rules consistently and using a system of written notices, a landlord shows tenants that he or she is in control and that no one receives special treatment. Good tenants will be encouraged to stay when they know that lease terms about rent payment and rules about noise, trash disposal, parking, and other matters apply equally to everyone in the building. They will view this consistency as one of the positive aspects of living in the landlord's building.

Other Tenant Indiscretions

Some tenants like to play music long after it is reasonably tolerated by others in the building or nearby houses. Other tenants may decide to keep a pet snake, even if the lease prohibits all types of pets.

When a tenant is in breach of the landlord's rules or the landlord/tenant laws of the state, the same notice procedure that applies to the late payment or nonpayment of rent should be employed.

Habitability

Every state requires that residences be habitable, meaning that they are in proper condition for occupancy. Sometimes landlords make the mistake of allowing a tenant to move into an apartment that is not completely habitable and charging a lower rent to compensate for not bringing the apartment up to habitability standards. The tenant can report the deficiencies to the proper authorities, which will force the landlord to fix the problems.

Landlords must understand that any appliances and systems in the unit, such as air conditioners, must be in working order when a tenant takes over the unit. If, for example, a humidifier in a unit is broken and the landlord does not want to repair or replace it, he or she should remove it before showing the unit to prospective tenants.

Informing Tenants of Disruptions

Tenants dislike having their privacy and routines disrupted unexpectedly. If a landlord plans to undertake major repairs at a property, such as replacing the roof or the siding, he or she should inform the tenants that workers will be on the premises for a specific amount of time and that there will be noise.

Evictions

Landlords must understand how the eviction process works in the jurisdiction in which their properties are located. This involves knowing what forms to fill out, where and when to submit them, which supporting documents to include, how much the filing fees are, and how the court papers must be served on the defaulting tenant. It is also a good idea for new landlords to spend some time observing court proceedings to familiarize themselves with the protocol involved.

Although the eviction process is an available tool for the removal of tenants who are or become undesirable, landlords will find that it is expensive and time consuming. For these reasons, landlords should try other methods of getting the tenants out before resorting to eviction. In other words, a landlord should find out what it will take to get a tenant to move. It may be that the tenant needs help moving to another location or finding another apartment. Perhaps the tenant needs to find somewhere to store personal items. The few dollars and little time that a landlord spends to help the tenant move out voluntarily is a miniscule price to pay compared with the eviction process.

Increasing the Rent

As the cost of operating a rental property goes up, there will be a need to raise the rent. You do not want to curtail the cash flow and suppress the value of your property by keeping the rents unreasonably low. You may hesitate about raising rents for fear that your tenants will move out. This fear by and large is unfounded, because tenants expect their rents to go up by a reasonable amount.

Nonetheless, before raising the rent, you need to find out what the rental market is doing in the area where your property is located. If the market is taking off, you can raise the rents; because the new rent you are charging will be in line with the other rents in the area, the tenants will have no good reason to disrupt their lives by moving. If the market has softened, the wiser course may be to forego a rent increase for the time being; you do not want to stir up your tenants unnecessarily, encourage vacancies, and have to find new tenants.

If you find that the rental market supports an increase, let your tenants know the reasons for the increase. In your notice of the rent increase, you can include a copy of your survey of the area rental market and inform them how much, in percentage terms, the real property taxes, insurance, and maintenance expenses have risen since the last rent increase.

You can train your tenants to expect modest but regular rent increases if you implement the increases at the same time each year. This can mean raising the rent one unit at a time as the lease comes up for renewal, or all at once on all the units.

Some experts suggest that a landlord can ease the blow of a rent increase by performing modest upgrades to a property, such as washing the outside of the windows or steam-cleaning carpets in one or two rooms in the units. Other experts dismiss this as an unnecessary expense, particularly if the landlord has not been deferring the maintenance. Still, other experts suggest upgrades to units as a way to justify rent increases where the rent is already at market level.

When Tenants Leave

Eventually, a tenant will want to move out at the end of his or her lease term. The lease should specify the amount of time that a tenant has to notify you in writing that he or she does not intend to renew the lease; it is often 30 days before the expiration of the lease. The landlord needs this advance warning to start planning for the repair or upgrade of the unit and obtaining a new tenant, preferably from a waiting list of prospects who already have been screened.

Before the tenant moves out, the landlord must arrange to do a final walkthrough of the unit. The landlord, together with the tenant, can then compare the condition of the unit with photographs, a checklist, or other method used to document the condition of the unit at the start of the tenancy.

The way to avoid problems with the tenant over the condition of the property is not to try to pass on to the tenant the cost of maintenance that the landlord failed to perform during the tenancy or to overcharge for the cost of making repairs in the unit. A landlord must not view the tenants' security deposits as a way to make extra money. Instead, a landlord should make deductions from a security deposit only when necessary to cover the cost of repairing or replacing an item that should not have broken in the course of normal wear and tear; for example, windows or faucets do not break on their own. The tenant is less likely to balk at deductions from the security deposit for such costs if the landlord has acted fairly throughout the tenancy.

As for the expense of cleaning an apartment when a tenant vacates it, some experts in property management recommend that landlords view this as a normal cost of doing business and that they refrain from charging tenants for it. Tenants who believe that a landlord has unfairly deducted a cleaning charge from their security deposits may take a landlord to court and almost certainly will tell other people that their former landlord was unscrupulous.

Fairness Goes Far

As a landlord, your responsibility is to provide your tenants with well-maintained units in exchange for the timely payment of rent. As in any commercial endeavor, you also have the responsibility to treat tenants — your clients — fairly. This is a sound business principle because you want their "repeat business" in the sense that you want good tenants to live in your units for extended periods of time as well as a reputation as a fair and professional landlord.

19

THE MANAGEMENT
OF PROPERTIES

Owners of residential properties who treat their investment activities as a business understand that their tenants are their customers and that the commodities for which those customers pay are the rental units. Having accepted this premise, owners also must accept responsibility for providing the commodity in the best shape possible under prevailing market conditions and repair and upgrade the commodity to enhance its value.

This means that an investor who buys a rental property must quickly implement a system for routine maintenance and emergency repairs. The tenants also should be informed of the proper procedures for reporting the need for emergency and nonemergency repairs in their units.

Being a good businessperson also means being constantly on the lookout for new sources of revenue production and ways to keep operating expenses in check.

Routine Maintenance

Landlords must maintain their rental houses, mobile homes, or mobile-home parks. This will involve taking routine preventive and corrective measures.

Custodial Measures

Unless the landlord plans to do the work personally, he or she will need to hire a custodial-type worker or subcontractor to pick up trash around the outside of a building, mow the lawn, prune shrubs, maintain the back yard, wash the outside of the windows, and broom-clean the common stairs and porch, if applicable. Depending on the configuration and rules of a building and the number of units in it, the custodial worker also may need to take the trash cans and recycling bins to the curb for pickup on the appropriate days of the week and return them to their rightful place after curbside pickup. Neatness and cleanliness go a long way toward making tenants feel proud and comfortable about the place where they live and giving passersby the impression of a well-maintained property.

Cosmetic Measures

To prevent a property from looking run down, a landlord must periodically inspect the grounds, the common areas, and the individual units for signs of wear and tear. These signs include chipped or peeling paint; burnt countertops; stained carpeting; chipped or cracked cement in the outside steps, foundation, or sidewalks; and dead or dying vegetation. These are conditions that require a watchful eye and consistent maintenance.

One of the least expensive measures to improve the appearance of a unit is to periodically steam clean the carpets. Frequent cleaning removes the dirt and enhances the color and also prolongs the life of the carpet. Thus, the minimal expenditure for regular maintenance saves money in the long run by postponing the need to replace the carpet.

The same is true with many other components of a property. Annual cleaning and maintenance of the furnace and air-conditioning system extend the years of service that can be expected of them. Stemming water leaks, whether from the roof or crevices in the basement, will prevent serious water damage and the infestation of mold. Landlords have to be particularly vigilant of mold, because insurance companies can readily blacklist properties that they identify as problematic for mold.

Nevertheless, eventually the carpeting will have to be replaced because cleaning will no longer be enough. This represents a substantial capital improvement, and the landlord should be able to increase the rent of the affected unit(s) to cover the cost. Some experts suggest that the recovery period for the cost of carpeting is three years. Therefore, if we assume that the cost of replacement carpeting is $1,500, the amount by which a tenant's monthly rent could be raised would be calculated as follows:

$1,500 (cost of carpet) ÷ 36 months (recovery period) = $42 per month

A landlord may have to adjust the $42 figure lower if the market where the property is located or the landlord/tenant laws of the jurisdiction do not allow the rent to rise by that much. To save money, a landlord can instead change the carpeting in only one or two rooms and clean the carpeting in the remaining rooms of a unit.

Similarly, a landlord will have to determine whether it is time to replace vinyl or linoleum flooring when cleaning no longer improves its appearance. The material itself is not costly, but the installation drives up the total price. In deciding whether to replace the flooring, the landlord must consider that vinyl or linoleum flooring, if maintained properly, will last for many years. The landlord also must consider whether changing the flooring will contribute to prolonging the tenants' stay in the affected units. A nominal rent increase should follow a replacement of vinyl or linoleum flooring.

A landlord should engage in the same type of reasoning when weighing the decision of whether to paint the common areas and individual units.

Kim McGregor, who invests in duplexes in Texas, suggested one way to save money on minor repairs:

"If there is a nearby property that has full-time maintenance people, figure out a way to talk to those people and see if any of them want to moonlight. You do not want to take anything away from their main job. Just ask if they can fix faucets and the like for you in the evenings or weekends, rather than you having to call a plumber."

Security/Safety Measures

Burnt-out light bulbs, inadequate lighting in common areas, broken stairs, damaged locks, cracked windows, broken or missing window latches, and damaged or inappropriate doors can compromise the security and safety of tenants. Tenant safety also is a concern if smoke alarms, fire extinguishers, or carbon monoxide monitors malfunction or are missing. Some states require fire escapes for residential properties in which tenants live on the third floor or higher; in such a case, the fire escape must be readily operational.

Improved Cash Flow = Increased Value

Every $1,000 of net operating income that an investor adds to residential real estate improves the value of the property by $10,000 to $12,000, and every $1,000 eliminated from the operating expenses also enhances the value of the property by $10,000 to $12,000. Because markets and tenant segments change, the investor who is best poised to succeed is the one who consistently refines his or her marketing strategies and management policies to adapt to market developments and the preference changes of the tenant segment that he or she serves.

In terms of dollars and cents, this means that investors must be on the lookout for ways to improve the cash flow of their properties. It also means making capital improvements when needed.

Enhance the Income Stream

The most common way to improve cash flow is to increase the rents consistently and periodically, as market conditions allow. Even a small rent increase improves the value of a property. This becomes evident with the use of the gross rent multiplier (GRM), which is one approach taken by appraisers to estimate the value of a rental property. The GRM is the ratio of income (total annual rents) to the price of a property. By comparing the GRMs of particular areas, an investor can roughly calculate what the price of a rental property should be.

Assume that Laurie Landlord purchased a triplex for $200,000. On monthly rents of $700, $700, and $800, Laurie collects total annual rents of $26,400. Based on these figures, the GRM of the property is calculated as follows:

> $200,000 (purchase price) ÷ $26,400 (total annual rents) = 7.6 GRM (rounded up)

If Laurie increased the rents the next year to $730, $730, and $840, the annual rents would rise by $1,200, for a new total of $27,600. The corresponding increase in the value of Laurie's property is calculated in this way:

> $27,600 (total annual rents) x 7.6 GRM = $209,760 (value of property)

With a small raise of $1,200 in annual rents, Laurie will make the market value of her property increase by more than $9,000 in just one year.

The GRM will vary from area to area, even neighborhood to neighborhood. The higher the GRM, the lower the cash flow and the higher the area incomes will be. Nonetheless, the precise meaning of various GRMs differs among experts. For example, some believe that a GRM of 6.1 to 9 indicates a middle-income to upper-middle-income area. In contrast, others say that a GRM of 6 to 7 indicates an area that is not "good," where appreciation is low even though the cash flow is high, and that a GRM of 8 to 11 indicates that a property is in satisfactory condition, has tolerable tenants, is in an adequate area, and can mean ample levels of cash flow and appreciation.

Increasing the rent is not the only way to increase the cash flow of a property. Chapter 11 examines different ways that the owner of a mobile-home park can create additional income streams. Similarly, owners of two- to four-family houses can develop new sources of income by installing coin-operated washers and dryers in the basement and providing extra storage, such as locked rooms or units in the basement, for a nominal fee. Current and future tenants will appreciate the convenience of having these facilities on site.

Sometimes the addition of an appliance is enough to increase the value of a unit on the rental market. Kim McGregor, who invests in duplexes in Texas, took that into consideration when he contracted to buy a duplex recently.

"In one of these duplexes that I have under contract, neither unit has a dishwasher, which are virtually required, or de rigeur, for anyone above a subsistence level in this market. I have a buddy who is really skilled. He and I can install one in four or five hours, modifying the cabinets, doing the plumbing and the wiring and the rest. That is what I will do if the units are vacant. In that way, I will create value so that the units will rent for more in the long run."

Reduce Operating Expenses

You may have heard the expression, "You have to spend money to make money." For owners of two- to four-family homes, mobile homes, or mobile-home parks, a more accurate adage is "You have to spend less money to make more money." This refers to improving the cash flow of a property by cutting the expenses of operating it.

One way to do this is to negotiate lower rates from handymen and service providers, such as electricians, plumbers, roofers, and furnace specialists. Another way is to find less expensive sources for paint, flooring, and other supplies and materials that are used frequently or in large quantities. Similarly, to pay lower premiums for insurance on the property, an owner may comparison shop for insurance, as long as the coverage is truly identical.

An owner may also consider having a local utility company conduct an energy audit of a building. If there are common areas for which the owner is responsible, the energy audit can reveal ways of reducing the energy bills for those areas, such as by replacing incandescent light bulbs with fluorescent ones and sealing doors and windows. Even if there are no common areas, an owner can have energy audits conducted in the units in a building to determine whether inexpensive insulation and other simple measures can help the tenants reduce their energy bills; the landlord can provide the tenants with the report generated by the utility company and can leave the suggested low cost improvements for the tenants to implement, as permitted by their leases.

In addition, consistent preventive maintenance can avert expensive measures in the future. This will require periodic inspections of the major components of a building, such as the roof and furnace. Landlords can ask the service professionals they use about replacing systems that are expensive to maintain with more efficient, lower-cost ones.

In properties for which the landlord pays the water bill, savings associated with water use can easily be realized by:

- Changing toilet flush valves

- Repairing dripping faucets

- Changing showerheads for low-flow water streams

If a management company is handling a property, the landlord should visit the property with a company representative and list the items that must be repaired or replaced, such as the front steps or a hot water heater, or activities that must be implemented, such as mowing the yard. Each task on the list should be scheduled for a specific date.

Pay Bills on Time

Timeliness with bills may seem an obvious measure, but bills for property taxes, water, and service providers frequently go unpaid for weeks, even months, beyond their due dates. This results in needless expense in the form of interest and penalties that are tacked on to the original bill.

For recurring annual or quarterly expenses, such as taxes and insurance, it is more efficient to divide the total annual bill by 12 and set aside that amount each month. This self-imposed escrow fund will be readily available to pay the bills when due. Automatic, electronic bill payment from a bank account is another way to avoid late payments and fees.

A self-imposed escrow is also a good way to save up for large maintenance or upgrade expenses that are anticipated. Thus, if it is November and the roof will need to be replaced in the spring, the landlord can obtain an estimate from a roofing contractor, divide the estimate figure by the number of months that remain before the work will be performed, and set aside that amount each month.

Reduce Property Taxes

Many municipal tax authorities reassess the value of properties within their borders every five to ten years. The rapid rise in property prices from 2002 to mid 2006 led to a corresponding rise in property taxes in some areas at about the same time that tax revenues from retail sales and commercial properties began to drop and enhanced homeland security measures in the wake of the September 11, 2001 attacks needed to be funded.

Now that prices of residential properties are sinking in many areas of the country, the basis of the higher taxes should be harder to justify. Local tax assessors are not able to figure out the precise assessment of each property. Instead, they make quick calculations that (1) can be thrown off by the sale of a few expensive properties in an area and (2) may not take into consideration the differences in characteristics and amenities that make one property more valuable than anther. By some estimates, 35 to 40 percent of all properties across the nation are over-assessed, but less than 5 percent of property owners appeal their assessments. Some experts say that about half of the taxpayers who do appeal succeed in obtaining a reduction in their assessments and, by extension, their property tax bills.

If you want to increase your cash flow, or at least prevent it from deteriorating from annual rises in the tax bill, consider challenging the tax assessment of your rental properties. A successful appeal requires establishing the true value of your property. You may do this for several hundreds of dollars by hiring a professional appraiser to review the data on recent sales of comparable properties in the area, make adjustments for the differences between those properties and yours, and defend the results to the tax authorities.

Alternatively, you can file your own tax appeal, if you are willing to do the necessary background work. There are several books that explain the process and give tips on how to present an appeal that has a chance of succeeding. Broadly speaking, you will:

- Obtain from a real estate agent a list of recent comparable sales in the area

- Review the comparables for recent renovations, decking, landscaping, and other features that make the sold properties more valuable than your property

- List the problems with your property, such as an old furnace or a lack of closet space or dishwasher that a tax assessor would not be able to see while driving by your property

- Apply the statutory assessment ratio to your determination of fair market value and compare that result with the figure used by the tax assessor

If you find that there is a substantial difference in your favor, you have grounds for a tax appeal, and you can contact the county tax assessment office for the form and procedures for making the appeal.

Preparing for a tax appeal is more involved than described above, so it is advisable to consult materials that focus on the tax-appeal process, talk to other taxpayers who have successfully challenged their assessments, and consult tax-appeal experts, if possible.

The time to file a tax appeal is relatively short; often it is April 1 of the current tax year. Check your tax bill for the deadline for filing appeals.

Keep Pristine Records

A good businessperson knows how much the business takes in and how much it pays out. For an owner of rental properties — even those that are managed professionally — it is essential that the record keeping be accurate and complete. This will give the owner insight into how the investment is faring and will serve as an effective defensive measure if the IRS ever audits the owner or challenges representations made about the income or expenses of the property.

20

SELF-MANAGE
OR HIRE MANAGEMENT?

The management of a rental property is a multifaceted endeavor. Concerning tenants, management involves:

- Screening and selecting tenants

- Collecting rents

- Fielding tenant complaints

- Handling lease renewals

- Notifying tenants of and implementing rent increases

- Evicting tenants who breach their leases

- Advertising for new tenants

- Showing units to prospective tenants

Concerning the property itself, management includes:

- Arranging for repairs, painting, cleaning, and other maintenance to units, the property exterior, and the major systems of the property

- Arranging for the upkeep of the front and back yards

- Paying contractors and others who perform services at the property

- Scheduling inspections of the property, as required by government entities

- Accounting for the rents collected and expenses paid

- Paying the bills for property taxes, insurance, sewer, and other recurring expenses

As these lists show, there are many duties involved in operating a rental property. These duties increase exponentially with each additional multiunit property purchased. An investor must determine whether he or she should handle all the duties or hire a professional property manager to perform all or some of them.

Kim McGregor is a full-time commercial property manager who invests in duplexes. This is how he handled the management of duplexes that he bought in a town that is one hour from his Austin, Texas, home:

"I was managing them myself on my trips up there every two weeks or so. When I had acquired more than 20 units, it got to be a little cumbersome, and I wasn't doing an adequate job. I tried using someone on site, but that did not work out. Eventually, I found a company in that small town that does a good job. I'm paying a rather heavy price, but the company is doing a better job than I was, so it is worth the price. I am still involved in many decisions regarding the properties."

Self-Managing Your Property

Novice landlords may want to self-manage their first few multiunit properties. The benefits to doing so include saving money on management fees, renting vacant units more quickly, learning about the rental market, and gaining firsthand experience of the day-to-day operations.

Notwithstanding those attractive benefits, not all investors have the time, ability, and drive to learn on their own how to manage rental properties.

Prudent first-time landlords should ask themselves the following questions when deciding whether to self-manage their rental properties:

- Do I want to commit the time and effort required?

- Do I like dealing with people and solving problems?

- Can I respond to tenant complaints and requests for service in an even-keeled, rational manner?

- Am I capable of handling basic accounting duties and paperwork and keeping good records?

- Do I possess maintenance and repair skills, or can I find capable contractors and handymen and oversee their work?

- Am I willing to work evenings and weekends, if needed, and to accept phone calls at all hours of the day and night?

- How good are the sales and negotiations skills that I will need to convince prospective tenants to rent from me and contractors and handymen to work for me, all on terms that are favorable to me?

- Do I have the patience to deal with the documentation requirements and red tape of government agencies?

- Will all the time and energy I devote to managing the properties inhibit my ability to find and buy more investment properties?

An investor who has a full-time profession in another field, is self-employed, or runs a business that is not related to property management will have to think carefully about the additional demands on his or her time that will be involved in self-managing rental properties.

Professional Property Managers

If an investor decides that he or she lacks the patience, temperament, or interest to self-manage rental properties, he or she must be prepared to delegate the management duties to someone else and to pay for the services rendered. The investor can choose how much management responsibility to retain; for example, the investor may want to personally collect the rents and deal directly with the tenants or to see to the upkeep and improvement of the properties.

Some landlords offer free or reduced-rent apartments to on-site caretakers who handle some of the day-to-day routines, such as basic maintenance chores, showing and renting vacant apartments, and dealing with contractors and others who work at the property. When using caretakers, the landlords retain as much responsibility as they want, such as for advertising rentals and setting the rules for tenants. Using caretakers who pay little or no rent may not be practical for an investor with a small building that produces little cash flow.

A landlord who wants to be more passive, and who finds that it is financially feasible, can hire a property management company to handle all aspects of operating a rental property. Management companies can provide benefits by:

- Saving the landlord time and effort

- Having and applying valuable insight into the local rental market

- Having effective policies and procedures that they have developed over time for various aspects of managing properties, such as screening tenants, lining up tradespeople for maintenance work, and getting rid of deadbeat tenants

- Reporting to the landlord about the state of the property, necessary major capital improvements, and tenancy matters that require attention

Nonetheless, there are at least two main drawbacks to using management companies. First, a management company that handles hundreds of rentals for numerous owners is unlikely to custom-design a strategy for boosting the profit potential of any one property. Second, management companies may charge a monthly fee of 6 to 10 percent of the monthly rent collections, depending on the size of the property; the smaller the property, the higher the percentage of the fee taken by a management company. Some management companies charge a flat monthly fee, and others will not consider handling a property with fewer than five rental units.

A fee based on a percentage of the monthly rents collected may give a management company two incentives: (1) to collect the rents and (2) to prevent the rents from dipping below market rates. Some management companies may tack on additional fees for renting vacant units, evicting tenants, and arranging for repairs.

Bad management companies cost landlords profits, not only with their fees, but also by renting units to tenants of poor quality and failing to properly maintain the properties.

Lisa Moren-Bromma is president of The Entrust Group, which is a third-party administrator of self-directed retirement plans. She also invests in real estate thousands of miles from her California home.

"I got to a point where doing the Entrust business and trying to manage was just not making sense. One of the people from whom I bought property in Florida introduced me to someone with 30 years of property management experience, and I ended up hiring him to manage my property in that one area. In another area, I tried to do it myself, and it was a disaster. So I hired a real estate company to do it and learned the hard way you don't do that either. Then I bartered with a tenant to manage the property and I discounted her rent, but that ended up being an even worse fiasco. So now I have a professional property management company handling the property. It is not easy when you buy from afar."

How to Find a Good Management Company

When you find the names of several property management companies, such as through recommendations from real estate agents or other landlords, plan on visiting the companies personally. You will want to speak with the managers who would be handling your property and ask them about their experience with your type of property, how many properties they are handling, their success rate in collecting rents and getting rid of bad tenants, and how quickly they fill vacant units. Ask not only for references, but also for a list of their clients. You should speak with the clients who have properties that are comparable to yours and ask whether they are satisfied with the services provided by the management company.

Many real estate sales offices provide property management services, but experienced investors recommend using the services of companies that are devoted only to the management of properties and do not do it as a sideline.

Landlords should inquire about the licenses, if any, required by many states for property managers, as well as the professional certificates and credentials of the management company being considered. These credentials may include the Certified Property Manager and Accredited Residential Manager designations bestowed by the Institute of Real Estate Management. They may also include designations given from the trade group the National Association of Residential Property Managers. For more information, see **www.narpm.org**.

Other matters that landlords should look into include the size of the fidelity bond that the management company has posted to cover the embezzlement or misuse of funds by its employees and the types of insurance the company has, including for professional liability (also known as errors and omissions coverage). Additionally, a landlord should find out whether a management company maintains a separate account for each of the properties it manages, rather than having just one account that contains the funds of all its clients.

Many property management contracts allow a management company to handle emergency repairs and undertake nonemergency repairs up to a specific dollar amount, both without prior approval from the owner. An owner should set a reasonable limit on the cost of unapproved repairs based on the size of the property, such as $300 for a duplex. An owner will need to monitor the expenses incurred by the management company it selects, particularly at the beginning of the relationship, to see how quickly after undertaking a repair the company advises the owner about it and whether the charges for supplies, labor, and material are appropriate.

Part IV

BEYOND RENTAL PROPERTY

21

NAVIGATING IN GOVERNMENTAL WATERS

As the owner of rental property, sooner or later you will have to deal with a governing body or a government agency on matters that affect your property. The larger your property, or the grander your plans for it, the more frequent and potentially contentious your encounters with government authorities will be.

Those encounters can involve anything from fighting citations for insignificant code infractions to attending hearings before zoning and planning boards on applications to change the use or expand the footprint of a building.

Although some local governments leave owners of multifamily properties relatively in peace, others seem to exist just to heap restrictions on owners. Many times, owners of rental properties feel they are under siege by lawmakers.

The Triple Whammy

Owners of rental properties must answer to three "masters:" federal, state, and local governments. The federal government comes into play with its tax laws and, at times, with its environmental regulations. Additionally, the Section 8 rental assistance program, a creature of federal lawmakers, imposes its own set of rules and requirements, such as the annual inspection of units rented by Section 8 tenants.

The state government has its court system, environmental mandates, building and fire codes, and tax and landlord/tenant statutes. One of the most potent and potentially devastating actions that a state government can take is to exercise it power of eminent domain, which allows it to take over private property, traditionally for public purposes. Only a handful of states have passed legislation to overcome a 2005 U.S. Supreme Court ruling that allows a state or local government to use eminent domain to take away private properties and turn them over to private developers if greater taxes and economic benefits will result.

The local government is the entity with which landlords will have the most contact. Local governments have their zoning regulations and health, safety, and building codes. When a property fails to meet current zoning or building codes, the owner may be in technical violation of the applicable code. If the condition existed before the code was enacted or revised and the building complied with the code before it was changed, the owner may not have to retrofit or upgrade the building to meet the new requirements; this is known as grandfathering. Most states do not permit grandfathering regarding fire codes.

If you own a rental property and want to create an additional unit in it, you will need to apply to the local planning and zoning boards for a zoning variance and other permissions. You will have to submit plans, drawings, and other documents to support your application and listen to comments from members of the community. This is a broad description of an involved, time consuming, and often expensive process.

Challenges Encountered by Owners

Laws vary from state to state, and even city to city within a state. In addition, some laws apply to rental properties of one size but not another. Investors who are determined to succeed must learn to fight in challenging situations.

Over-Regulation

Investor Anna Mills of Toledo, Ohio, is well-informed about her state and local laws and their effect on her ownership of rental properties.

"The State of Ohio has 134 statutes on the books to be discussed this year just dealing with real estate. This does not include the local laws, which are starting to get really crazy. For instance, Cincinnati has an ordinance which states that if there are truant children in your building, you, the landlord, can go to jail. Toledo just passed the "party law:" if your tenants party, you can go to jail. That is a good way to not pay the rent — throw a party and get your landlord thrown in jail. Also in Toledo, landlords are not allowed to rent to three or more unrelated people. Yet, the federal Fair Housing Act says you cannot even ask applicants about family status. We took Toledo to the Ohio Supreme Court over that, and Toledo took the law off its books the week the case was to be heard. Three months after the case was dropped from the court docket, the city put the law back on the books."

Richard Seltzer, an investor in residential properties in New Jersey, noted that federal lawmakers changed the U.S. Tax Code in 1986 to "clamp down" on the number of people who were investing in real estate and taking advantage of the many tax benefits that were available. He says that landlords face "endless" challenges when dealing with the government:

"Municipal government obstacles, state government obstacles, and on the federal level, things like changes in the tax code — the obstacles can be extreme. The governments change the building codes, the fire codes, they want bribes from you, and they even ticket you for not putting the recycling in the proper bins."

Mills said she has seen her share of uneven code enforcement. "There can be houses all over the area that are boarded up, falling down, gutters coming off, and you have a crack in a step or a downspout that doesn't have a little curve on the end of it, and you're the one who gets ticketed," she noted.

The Meat Cleaver Approach

Rebecca McLean, executive director of the National Real Estate Investors Association, said she is also troubled by the approach taken by many local governing bodies.

"What tends to happen is as true in investing as it is in anything else. One bad apple spoils the whole bunch. When an investor participates in a bad business practice, someone panics, and instead of using the law that is on the books — and almost always there is something that could be enforced against the person — the city council is up in arms about the matter and makes up a new law to show the community that it is taking action. Many times, the new law is quite onerous and not only bad for the investor, but for the community at large, if the lawmakers actually looked at the long-term consequences. Unfortunately, they go right on trying to fix short-term problems with something that, down the road, is going to be a problem for the whole community."

As an example, McLean noted there have been cases in which property owners facing foreclosure have been swindled in lease/option deals offered by unscrupulous investors. According to McLean, "Many states have reacted by trying to make it difficult for investors to work with people in foreclosure. Lawmakers have decided that if that is going to be the problem, they will take the lease/option choice away." The problem with this approach, said McLean, is, "with fewer choices at their disposal, people facing foreclosure will end up losing their homes and suffering a major hit to their credit. In trying to protect those who have been taken advantage of by one or two people, lawmakers have left the multitudes of homeowners without the help they need."

Fines as Cash Cows

Investor Anna Mills believes she has an explanation for the fines and penalties levied by government regulators.

"As the government needs more and more money, all these rules and regulations are just for the fines, because the government perceives you, the landlord, as having deep pockets. It never crosses the minds of the lawmakers that you are their tax base. In any city and town in America, the landlords are the largest small business, but they are never looked at that way by the regulators. The more a government puts landlords out of business, the smaller the tax base, and there goes affordable housing."

John Hyre, who invests in mobile-home parks, also noted that some municipalities charge high prices for water and other services as "a tax collecting method."

Interstate Complexities for Mobile Homes and Parks

Those who invest in mobile homes and mobile-home parks have their own set of challenges in dealing with government regulators.

David Reynolds of Colorado has invested in both mobile homes and mobile-home parks. Relating to the sale of mobile homes, he is familiar with the licensing requirement imposed by some states on persons who sell more than a specified number of units in one year.

"In Texas, if you buy and sell more than one mobile home a year, you must go to three days of classes in Austin, put up a bond just like a car dealer, and then you become a licensed mobile-home dealer. The specific requirements vary from state to state. In some states, the limit is two mobile homes, in others, three, and in some others, you can get away with more than that, as long as it is not an ongoing type of business."

Reynolds cautioned that it is not a good idea to try to bypass the licensing laws. "If you are supposed to be a dealer, and the state finds out that you are not licensed, it will fine you. Plus, if someone buys a mobile home from you, then does not like it, the state can make you reimburse the purchase price to the buyer and sometimes even two to three times that amount. So a $10,000 sale could cost you $30,000."

Zoning laws often hinder the development of new mobile-home parks. As Reynolds noted:

"With any kind of property, you must have the proper zoning, get a variance, or have the property rezoned. There are very few properties that have the proper zoning for new mobile-home parks. You might find a piece of property and think it would be a great place for a park. By the time you could actually get the zoning, permits, engineering, and the rest, you might be into the deal for a year or two and have $50,000 in all those costs for plats and zoning and engineering fees. So it is not an easy process to start a new park. It is much simpler to buy an existing park and expand it."

Hyre, an Ohio resident who owns a small mobile-home park in Indiana, said he finds that updated laws often hinder his ability to act like a prudent businessman.

"When I walk through a park and I see a rusted-out metal, pre-1976, 12-foot by 60-foot mobile home, it is worth less than zero to me. I would have to get rid of who is in it, pay someone to haul it away, and if I have a grandfather issue on the lot, it creates an even bigger problem. For example, in Ohio, if I pull a mobile home from a lot, the law that applies to the lot changes to modern law, and it may be physically impossible to comply with the law, so I may not be able to move the home. In Indiana, they are more laid back. As long as you can show that you are going to make the park better, they usually are not going to give you a hard time."

Hyre also said, "I would not buy a mobile-home park that has well water, especially not in a high-regulation state like Ohio, because the local environmental protection agencies can shut the park down at the drop of a hat over water issues."

There is also the matter of periodic inspections of mobile-home parks. As Reynolds explained:

"Every state is different. Sometimes, the inspectors come from the state level, sometimes they come from a county or city level. In Illinois, the state health department comes out every year and does a walk through my park and writes up any issues. Same thing for Wisconsin, where every year the state health department comes out and goes through lot by lot, home by home, and writes down every issue and gives the report to the park owner to correct the issues or have the residents correct them. Not every state has them, but I would say about half of them do annual inspections and require a license fee. The main things the inspectors look for are junk cars, yards full of junk, trash or lumber, fire hazards. It could be lighting in the streets. Streets are usually a big consideration, such as whether they have big potholes."

Staying Afloat

These anecdotes from experienced investors are not meant to sink the hopes and enthusiasm of new investors or owners of single-family homes who want to make the leap into multiunit properties, mobile homes, or mobile-home parks. The point is to stress the need to have more than a passing familiarity with the federal and state laws and local codes that may apply to your properties.

Regarding government conflict on the road to investment success, Richard Seltzer said, "You have to avoid it as much as you can. You can't fight city hall. You have to know the rules, and don't bother trying to challenge them. Just grit your teeth and comply with them as efficiently and inexpensively as possible."

On the other hand, investors such as Anna Mills and organizations such as the National Real Estate Investors Association and various apartment owners' groups prefer to band together to encourage the passage of landlord-friendly legislation and to try to strike down laws that overreach, are too burdensome, and are badly thought-out.

CONCLUSION

By reading this entire book, you have gained more than a passing familiarity with the essential principles of successfully investing in residential properties such as duplexes, triplexes, fourplexes, mobile homes, and mobile-home parks. Congratulations. You have demonstrated to yourself that you are serious about heading in an exciting, rewarding direction.

What You Have Learned So Far

To sum up in broad terms, this is what you have learned from the preceding chapters:

- You need an investment plan that sets financial targets, a purchase schedule, and an exit strategy

- Assemble your team of experts

- Choose the right form of ownership for your protection

- You must do your homework before shopping for specific investment properties

- After finding one or more properties that seem promising, you must independently verify, as much as possible, the representations made about the properties

- After entering into a contract to buy a property, due diligence is indispensable

- Properly screen the people who want to rent units from you

- Demonstrate leadership as you manage your tenants, and treat them fairly

- Manage your properties prudently to increase their value

- Know when to sell

- Do not be surprised if you find yourself leveraging your knowledge and expanding into other investment vehicles

Above all else, you now understand that investing in residential properties is a business in which you have tremendous control over the amount of risk to which you want to be exposed. It is entirely up to you to decide whether the business is big or small, how many properties to own, and whether to manage personally or with professional help.

There are a few other items you need to know that come with the territory of investing in rental properties.

Money is Not the Sole Reward

Many investors begin by buying a two-family house and renting one of the units while living and raising a family in the other. With the confidence gained as landlords on this small scale, they later branch out and start buying and renting more properties. It is not just about the money — they learn to enjoy investing in rental properties and marvel at their growing ability to handle the challenges that go with it.

Anna Mills of Toledo, Ohio, is a good example of this. She became a real estate agent more than 30 years ago, when it was rare for a woman to do so. Within a year of obtaining her license, she began investing in residential real estate.

"I acquired the first house by taking over the payments. I would assume loans and let the people stay in the houses until they could find another house or were transferred by their jobs or whatever they had to do. They in turn got the mortgage off their names, which allowed them to qualify to move or buy something else. Just by helping out my own clients, I started finding houses. I now have 27 single-family homes, and I still manage my own properties. I also manage my business partner's fourplexes. He started investing last year and already has about 12 units. I enjoy doing something different every day, I guess because I can."

Kim McGregor of Austin, Texas, began managing apartments while he was still in college. He now works for a real estate company, where he manages office buildings and shopping centers. McGregor also used to manage fourplexes for another investor. These daytime activities did not deter McGregor from pursuing his own real estate investments.

"The first house I ever bought had a garage apartment with it. We [he and his wife] lived in the house for several years and rented out that apartment. I liked the way that worked out, and then about 30 years ago, I bought another house, lived in it a while, and bought another one and rented out the previous one. I did that two or three times. That is how I got started, by renting out the house that I lived in and buying another one."

By McGregor's own admission, he became "duplex crazy" over the years.

He started buying several at a time, managing all of them himself at first. "I'm addicted, I guess. I do not get enough real estate during the daytime, so I have my own at night," he said. His personal real estate portfolio now includes about 32 rental properties, although that number fluctuates as he sells and buys through 1031 exchanges. "I promised my wife several times that this or that was my last deal, but it never has been. She does not believe me any more," McGregor said.

About 26 years ago, attorney Richard Seltzer began investing in multifamily housing in Hoboken, New Jersey. Here is his explanation why:

"Hoboken was undervalued then, and I saw its intrinsic value as a place to invest. Plus, at that time, I was interested in being a landlord and seeing what that was like, experimenting, seeing how hard it was. It seemed like a simple part-time job."

When Seltzer arrived in Hoboken, it was run down with a pier in shambles. Within ten years, Hoboken had polished its image, developed its waterfront — with a spectacular view of the New York skyline — and become a magnet for New Yorkers who saw that they could buy much more living space for their dollars there than in the Big Apple. Hoboken was developed to the hilt, and the prices of properties skyrocketed. Due to their proximity to Wall Street and other points in lower Manhattan, Hoboken and its surroundings have retained much of their value, even in the challenging real estate market of today.

Over the years, Seltzer invested in rental properties ranging from single-family houses to 40-unit buildings in Hoboken, Jersey City, and other areas. The properties have allowed him to be creative in his exit strategy, and he is pleased with his choices.

"The rewards have far outweighed the risks. It has been an extremely fortunate experience for me… The first building we [he and his partners] bought was a 10-family building for $76,000. This meant that the base price was $7,600 per apartment. We converted the units to condominiums in 1986 and started selling them for $40,000 to $80,000 each. It took ten years to do it, but that was the plan."

Mills, McGregor, and Seltzer have found divergent niches in vastly different areas of the country. What these and other experienced investors in residential properties have in common is a sense of enjoyment, satisfaction, and passion fueled by their investment careers.

Keep Learning

Of course, it is essential to learn all you can before buying your first investment property. After making your first investment, then your second and third, your experience will allow you to add to your knowledge bank.

Yet, do not rely solely on your experiences; keep learning from other sources. As McGregor suggested for those just starting out as investors:

"Get all of the expertise you can from other people that do it, not just from people that are selling the properties, but from people who have owned, managed, and sold them. If you are looking in a neighborhood and you see someone working on a unit or you see someone's 'For Rent' sign, call them up. They might be somebody just like you who has owned one or several units for a few years. I think if you catch them right, most people will be happy to share their experiences, both good and bad, with you."

How does one succeed in a chosen field? By selecting one small part of it and becoming an expert in it by learning as much as is possible about that small part. The same holds true for investing in rental properties.

David Reynolds is based in Colorado and has been investing in mobile-home parks throughout the United States for more than ten years. Experience has taught him to focus on one particular type of park.

"I concentrate on the 100- to 150-space mobile-home parks. That is my niche. I do not want to compete with the guys who are buying the real large properties at the low cap rates. So I focus on the ones that are smaller and out of their radar."

If you were to be as serious about investing in rental properties as you were about investing time and effort in acquiring the knowledge necessary for your profession, you would vastly increase your chances for success.

Ready, Set, Go

It may be that no one in your family or circle of friends and acquaintances invests in real estate. Perhaps some of them rent out a studio apartment over the garage or a room in the basement of their houses, but nothing more. You may be reluctant to be the one who breaks out of the mold in which everyone else around you is content to live.

Many of the most successful people in the arts, sciences, trades, and other fields have triumphed because they stepped out of their own way. They figured out that no matter how loudly and insistently the world proclaims certain people a "success," the only achievements that bring deep, personal joy and pride are those that individuals choose for themselves.

The gifted jazz musician and composer Chick Corea had this psychological truth in mind when he defined the formula for success as (1) deciding to do something and (2) doing it. He added that the rest of the equation consists of going about acquiring the knowledge necessary for the accomplishment of what one wants to do.

Corea's simple, elegant formula is the one followed by all the investors quoted in this book, even if they are not aware of it. You, too, can follow the formula and succeed. It comes down to deciding that you will invest in residential properties, learning all you can about how to do it intelligently, and then doing it.

You have taken a significant step on the road to success by reading this book. If you feel you need more knowledge, go out and get it. Just understand that there is only so much you can learn from books and other people's experiences. You will become a knowledgeable investor only when you invest. To do that, you will need to apply what you have learned and buy your first duplex, triplex, fourplex, mobile home, or mobile-home park.

BIBLIOGRAPHY

Berges, Steve, *The Complete Guide to Investing in Undervalued Properties.* (2005). New York: McGraw-Hill.

Consumer Federation of America and Wachovia Corp., "More Than Half of Americans Say They Are Not Saving Adequately." **www.consumerfed.org/pdfs/CFA_Wachovia_Savings_Press_ Release_12_10_07. pdf.**

Cummings, Jack, *Commercial Real Estate Investing.* (2005). Hoboken, New Jersey: John Wiley & Sons, Inc.

DeCima, Jay P., *Start Small, Profit Big in Real Estate.* (2005). New York: McGraw-Hill.

Department of Housing and Urban Development, "Bush Administration to Expand Mortgage Help for Struggling Families" Press release dated April 9, 2008. **www.hud.gov/news/release.cfm?content=pr08-050.cfm**

Donaldson, Corey, "Creating a Lifetime of Cash Flow and Equity through Mobile Home and Mobile-Home Park Investing." **www.mobilehomeuniversity.com**

Eldred, Gary W., *The Beginner's Guide to Real Estate Investing, 2d Ed.*, (2008). Hoboken, New Jersey: John Wiley & Sons, Inc.

Gallinelli, Frank, *Insider Secrets to Financing Your Real Estate Investments*. (2005). New York: McGraw-Hill.

Hart, John Fraser, Michelle J. Rhodes, and John T. Morgan, *The Unknown World of the Mobile Home*. (2002). Baltimore: The John Hopkins University Press.

Loftis, Larry B., *Investing in Duplexes, Triplexes & Quads*. (2006). New York: Kaplan Publishing.

Roth, Ken, *The Successful Landlord*. (2004). New York: AMACOM, a division of American Management Association.

Schaub, John W., *Building Wealth One House at a Time*. (2005). New York: McGraw-Hill.

Small Business Administration, Office of Advocacy, "The Small Business Economy for Data Year 2006: A Report to the President." **www.sba.gov/advo/research/sb_econ2007.pdf.**

Strauss, Spencer and Martin Stone, *The Unofficial Guide to Real Estate Investing, 2d Ed.*(2003). Hoboken, New Jersey: Wiley Publishing Co.

Tyson, Eric and Robert S. Griswold, *Real Estate Investing for Dummies*. (2005). Hoboken, New Jersey: Wiley Publishing Co.

Warr, Gregory D., *Make More Money Investing in Multiunits*. (2005). Chicago: Dearborn Trade Publishing, a Kaplan Professional company.

White, Bill J., *The National Consumer Law Center Guide to Mobile Homes*. (2002).Boston: The National Consumer Law Center.

About the Author

E.E. Mazier is a freelance writer, journalist, and real estate investor. Before retiring from the practice of law, she represented hundreds of individuals, partnerships, and corporations in real estate transactions. She has worked for the insurance magazine *National Underwriter-P&C*, and the newspapers *New Jersey Lawyer* and *The National Law Journal*. She is an award-winning short story writer, and her play Morrison, about Jim Morrison of the Doors, was showcased in an off-off Broadway production in 2001. She resides with her husband in New Jersey.

INDEX